100 IDEAS
FOR TEACHING
WRITING

CONTINUUM ONE HUNDREDS SERIES

100 IDEAS
FOR TEACHING
WRITING

Anthony Haynes

continuum

*To Gordon Boyd, who is
more concerned to theorise.*

Continuum International Publishing Group

The Tower Building   80 Maiden Lane, Suite 704
11 York Road   New York,
London   NY 10038
SE1 7NX

www.continuumbooks.com

British Library Cataloguing-in-Publication Data
A catalogue record for this book is available from the British
Library.

ISBN: 0826483097 (paperback)

Library of Congress Cataloging-in-Publication Data
Haynes, Anthony.
  100 ideas for teaching writing / Anthony Haynes.
    p. cm. -- (Continuum one hundreds series)
  ISBN-13: 978-0-8264-8309-6
  ISBN-10: 0-8264-8309-7
  1.   English language--composition and exercises--Study
and teaching. 2.   Effective teaching.   I. Title. II. Title: One
hundred ideas for teaching writing. III. Title: Hundred ideas
for teaching writing.   IV. Series.

  LB1576.H326 2007
  372.62'3--dc22

                                        2006029552

Designed and typeset by Ben Cracknell Studios
www.benstudios.co.uk

Printed and bound in Great Britain by Ashford Colour Press,
Gosport, Hampshire

CONTENTS

SECTION 4   The drafting process

SECTION 5 The redrafting process

SECTION 6 Completing the process

SECTION 7 Tasks

a) Setting tasks

b) Narrative

c) Argument

SECTION 9 **Assessment**

SECTION 10 **Resources and teacher development**

PREFACE

This book is designed to be read in two different ways. There is the dutiful approach – reading the book from cover to cover, taking in all 100 ideas in sequence. Rather to my surprise, that is how the book was in fact written (more or less). And then there is the cormorant approach (very much my own when reading as a teacher) in which you dip in here and there, every now and then, looking for one idea at a time.

A word to the cormorants among you. Although each idea will, I trust, make sense when taken in isolation, its full value will in many cases depend on the context provided by other ideas in the book. I suggest that in between dipping you look at least at the first eleven ideas in the book, which are the most general. Although those eleven won't give you ideas for particular lessons, they are designed to illuminate the other ideas in the book.

Whichever way you choose to read this book, it will help to understand its overall structure. Ideas have been grouped into sections, the headings for which are for the most part self-explanatory. I should, however, add one point of clarification. The division of classroom ideas into two main types – one dealing with the process of writing, the other providing ideas for tasks, is for the sake of clarity only. The book will prove of most benefit to those teachers who *combine* ideas of both types.

My thanks are due to Christina Garbutt and Karen Haynes for their professional guidance and to Frances Haynes for her advice and criticism.

General ideas

WRITING AND LINGUISTIC DEVELOPMENT

Writing is a mode of language use. How pupils' writing develops is comparable to the way their linguistic ability develops in other modes – speaking, listening, and reading. Their writing tends to develop better when it is interrelated to their general linguistic development, rather than treated as something separate. This would be obvious, were it not for aspects of our education system (separate assessment objectives, for example) that make us forget it.

In your lesson planning, ensure that you build bridges between language modes to help your pupils transfer their learning from one mode to another. Usually this involves setting work in other modes *before* the pupils write. For example, discussion in small groups (a much neglected form of preparatory activity) can help pupils to clarify and sequence ideas before expressing them on paper. But look out for opportunities to reverse the sequence. Pupils who have to give formal presentations, for example, are likely to want to write texts – or at least notes – first.

Whichever sequence you use, the important point is to make bridges between language modes central to your planning.

In Idea 1 I mentioned four modes of language use – writing, reading, speaking, listening. There is of course a fifth – thinking. We often use language subvocally, even subconsciously, as a way of processing our thoughts.

What has been said about the other four modes of language – that in the classroom they should be interrelated – applies, therefore, to thinking too. Unless you attend to this, there is a danger that pupils end up doing lots of busy work, looking industrious, covering paper, churning stuff out, but not really engaging or learning. The most (in)famous examples of this are those traditional comprehension exercises where sometimes – just by virtue of their grasp of the sentence structure of the text – students can correctly answer without ever understanding what the passage is about.

The best way to ensure that you build true thinking into the writing curriculum is to include cognitive as well as writerly terms in the assessment objectives and learning outcomes that you design. Verbs like 'question', 'contrast', 'imagine', 'apply', 'infer' and 'decide' and nouns like 'examples', 'evidence', 'assumption' and 'conclusion' help to pick out the thinking involved in writing.

PROGRESSION

The writing curriculum is to a large extent a spiral one: you can think of a pupil's writing development as a series of ever-widening (i.e. more skilful, more ambitious) circles in which the pupil revisits the same sectors (e.g. spelling, style, discourse structure) each term or each year.

Which is fine. But we do need to ensure that, each time our pupils return to some particular sector of the writing curriculum, the work stretches them and moves them on. Otherwise, there is a danger of a spiral curriculum becoming simply a circular one in which demands on the pupils are merely repeated. One of the primary school pupils in Jan Mark's novel, *Thunder and Lightnings* hands in the same project each year. I can remember myself having to draw a diagram of a blast furnace each year between the ages of about 8 and 14.

To ensure progression when constructing the curriculum, look both forward and back. Be sure to ask yourself how you can build on work that the pupils did last year and how you can prepare them for the work that they will need to do next year.

We use the word 'writing' to indicate both a product ('That essay is a good piece of writing') and a process ('I spent the afternoon writing'). Much time has been wasted discussing which type of writing in school is more important. They are both important, though neither of them is important all the time.

If a pupil is jotting down a few notes in preparation for writing a story, it is the process that matters. Provided the notes do their job, i.e. help the pupil to produce a good story, it doesn't matter how neat, legible, or grammatical they are. Who cares whether the notes are carefully punctuated – or punctuated at all?

If, on the other hand, the pupil has written a letter to be sent to a local councillor, a poem to be published in the school magazine, or a CV for a work placement, the business of dotting the 'i's and crossing the 't's matters enormously.

In each lesson you need to be clear in which sense you are concerned with 'writing'. Trying to focus on both simultaneously is like trying to aim with a single bow and arrow at two targets. Ask yourself, 'What is the point of this lesson? Is it to develop pupils as writers in some way (process) or is it to achieve a presentable artefact (product)?'

WRITING AS PRODUCT AND AS PROCESS

In his book *Writing and the Writer*, Frank Smith asks the reader to consider what happens when a book is written by an author dictating a book to a secretary. Who, he asks, is writing the book: the author or the secretary? In different ways, they both are. The author 'writes' the book in the sense of composing it – it is the author who comes up with the ideas, decides the diction, and formulates the syntax. The secretary 'writes' the book in the sense of transcribing it. It is the secretary who exerts the manual effort, attends to the orthography and punctuation, ensures legibility, and so on. Both the composing and the transcribing are, of course, essential. Without either, the book would not get written.

Writers, then, commonly adopt at least two roles – that of composer and that of transcriber. It is a central tenet of this book that we need to teach pupils both how to compose and how to transcribe.

It is also a central tenet that composition and transcription are different kinds of things and that it is best not to attend to both at the same time. When you're teaching composition techniques, focus on composition – transcription issues come later. And when you're teaching the secretarial aspects of writing, focus on transcription issues – leave composition out of the picture. That way you won't be asking your pupils to think about too many different kinds of thing all at the same time – neither will you burden yourself with worrying about every aspect of teaching writing all of the time.

Separating the two functions of writing, then, makes for both more clear-headed learning and more relaxed teaching. Can't be bad!

I'm sitting here, in my study, writing this book. In my file is a contract that requires me to write a certain number of words in a certain format by a certain date. To begin with, all of my energies are focused on my own concerns. How much time will it take? How can I fit it into my work schedule and my domestic routine (the children want me off the computer so they can use it)? What happens if I find I have only 97 ideas? Have I got all my favourite ideas in? How much room should I give to poetry? Please don't take offence, dear readers, but I'm not thinking of you just now.

But I will be. In fact, towards the end of the process, I will be thinking only of you. My questions then will be: Does that make sense? Is this passage clear enough? Is the range of ideas wide enough? Is the book sufficiently practical? Will someone just beginning to train as a teacher understand that? Will a reader from another country know what I mean? In this way my concerns will shift from those of the writer to those of the reader – which is typical of writing generally.

Vary your teaching according to the stage of the writing process that your pupils are working at. In the early stages of a writing assignment, help pupils to get stuff out of their heads and onto paper. Focus your advice on helping just to express it all. Later on, pose questions designed to put the pupils in the position of their reader(s). Concentrate on helping them to see their writing through a reader's eyes.

THE DEMANDS OF THE WRITER AND THOSE OF THE READER

WHO ARE WE WRITING FOR?

Because texts are read *after* they have been written, it is tempting to think of the reading and writing of texts as separate processes and to conclude, therefore, that the reader plays no part in the writing process. But in fact the question of readership affects writing from the very start of the process.

Supposing you are talking about the school you work in. Doesn't what you say (and the way you say it) depend on who you are speaking to? Wouldn't you talk differently according to whether you were talking to a pupil, parent, headteacher, inspector, colleague, friend, member of your family, journalist, etc? The same would be true if you were writing a description or account of it. The question of audience typically affects the choice of words, sentence structure, tone, selection of information, and so on.

In school we often make writing difficult for pupils by not specifying the audience. Just imagine how uncertain you'd feel if you were told to write a description of your school without being told who was going to read it.

To compound the problem, there is always one certain reader, namely the teacher. The problem here is that often the teacher already knows the information that the pupils' writing is designed to provide (indeed, might just have taught that information to those pupils). Ever felt frustrated that a pupil hasn't written enough, gone into enough detail, or explained things well enough? Well, sometimes the reason for that is simply that the pupil knows full well that you know the information already and can't see the point of telling you what you know.

Specify the audience. In particular, specify whether it is a personal one – some particular individual – or an impersonal one (as when you write a newspaper article or formal exam-style essay). Experiment with different audiences – either real ones (e.g. other pupils in the class, parents) or simulated ones (e.g. a character from a book or from history). For a list of possible audiences, see Idea 51.

Imagine you have to write an essay on the Second World War. What do you need to know before you can do it? You need information about the war itself – what happened, who did what, what the outcome was, and so on. But you also need to know what an essay is.

How do we learn what an essay is? And how do we learn what all the other genres we write in at school are – accounts, reports, letters, and so on? Well, sometimes the process is a bit hit and miss. The teacher gives some advice, your friends give you some tips, the teacher's marking provides some direction for next time round. What teachers sometimes do – but not always – is give the pupil models, i.e. examples of finished pieces of writing that they study and imitate.

Often the models we give pupils are professional ones. Coursework books and anthologies often provide examples of letters, diaries, journal entries, reports, and so on. This is fine. But what is also useful is to have some models written by pupils. Build up (with their permission of course) a bank of good examples of pupils' work to show to pupils in the future.

Note that subject matter is not what it's about. With the pupil writing an essay on the Second World War, you might not want to show them other essays on the same subject that might produce little more than plagiarism. But you might well want to show them essays by pupils on other historical subjects.

It's amazing how pupils' perplexity can disappear once they have a few models in front of them. 'Oh, I get it now, I see what you want!'

TEACHER AS ROLE MODEL

How much of your own writing do pupils get to read? How often do they see you writing – especially in a sustained way?

Pupils learn not just from what we tell them but also from what we do. Like it or not, we are role models. ('If s/he thinks writing is important, how come s/he never does any?') Try writing when they're writing. Try writing what they're writing. If you ask them to read some of their work out, try reading some of yours out too.

Think of writing as a series of overlapping processes of the following types:

1 Incubation
2 Planning and preparation
3 Drafting
4 Redrafting
5 Transcribing and checking
6 Presenting and publishing.

Some of these labels sound rather adult, but they apply even to the writing of young children. 'Publishing', for example, may mean simply posting a piece of work on the wall as a part of a display or reading it out in class.

These processes tend to be recursive. For example, while drafting a piece of writing, a writer might return to their plan and rethink it.

It is, of course, not necessary for each piece of writing to pass through each stage – still less to teach each stage each time. That would be extremely ponderous. It is a good idea, however, to consider (a) at which stages in the curriculum each process will be taught explicitly and (b) which processes are most appropriate to which pieces of work.

WRITING AS A PROCESS

IDEA

11

WHAT NOT TO DO

Don't use writing as a form of social control. Don't make the reason for setting writing be nothing more than a desire to get pupils' heads down. Or, rather, if you do, don't think that you can also teach that writing is a valuable, creative or wonderful activity.

And do not on any account ever use writing as a punishment. If any of your colleagues do that, persuade them not to!

The start of the process

INCUBATION

One of the most fascinating aspects of writing is the way that ideas and experiences incubate for a long time. The (auto)biographies of authors abound with examples of ideas or events that occur and then seem to disappear, only to surface in a piece of writing years, perhaps even decades, later. This process is one of the least understood aspects of the psychology of writing.

Unfortunately this is not of much help to teachers. It is unlikely that an inspector, wanting to know what the learning outcomes of a lesson were, will prove receptive to the idea of waiting for a few decades to find out.

There are some ways, however, in which you can harness the process of incubation. Teachers very often have a long-term plan for the academic year but often do not share it with pupils. It can help to flag up pieces of writing that pupils will be doing weeks or months ahead. It gives them an opportunity to think and to gather ideas. They may keep 'ideas journals' – for example, in the back of their exercise books – in which at regular times they jot down ideas that may later be developed into pieces of writing.

One stimulus for bringing submerged ideas to the forefront of the mind is a change of scene. For example, sometimes when we go away on holiday or to a conference we find ourselves thinking of something that hasn't occurred to us for years. I discovered the possibilities here purely by chance. One day at the start of a school field trip in France we found that the day's activities had finished too early, so I ran an impromptu creative writing session. I was surprised at how good the writing turned out to be, so we then ran an evening session each day that week.

One way to get started is to free-write. This is when pupils write and do nothing but write. The instruction should be, 'Write! Don't take your pen off the page, don't stop and think, don't look up!' Specify that you're not worried about quality, correctness, or neatness – you just want pupils to write. Assure pupils that they will not be required to read out their writing or show it to anyone.

Free-writing works best when it is for a very short and defined period of time – three minutes, say. It works even better when you make a point of joining in and doing the same as the pupils do. On some occasions you may wish not to specify a subject at all, on others you may wish to use it as the first stage of exploring some particular topic or theme.

The value of free-writing is that it overcomes inhibitions. It jolts people out of saying they can't think of anything to write.

Free-writing helps pupils to get ideas out of their heads and onto paper. They can then use what they have written as a prompt to contribute to discussion. They can also revisit what they have written and start turning it into something better. Free-writing is, therefore, a great way to begin teaching that writing is a process. For example, pupils might be asked to select a clause or sentence – or even just a word – from their free-written text and use it as the basis of a couple of sentences of more thoughtful, carefully shaped writing.

This idea comes from a book called *Let the Children Write*, written several decades ago by a teacher named Margaret Langdon. I love the book – and the writing it produces.

Point to a spider on the ceiling. It doesn't matter that there isn't really one there. Ham it up a bit: 'Wayne, what do you mean, you can't see it? You're not looking! Kevin, you can see it, can't you?' Make sure you've primed Kevin to agree with you.

Tell the pupils that now they've had a good look at the spider, you want to them to write one line (and one line only) about some specific aspect of it – its body, say. Then tell them to add another line on some other specified aspect – its legs, its colour ('Please don't any-one use the word "black"'), its web, the way it moves, and so on. Work one line at a time and always be specific. Finally ask them to read through what they've written and add one line to finish it off.

Pupils can produce surprisingly good pieces of writing like this. If you build it into classroom routine – perhaps once a week – it can become something that everyone looks forward to. You can generate large stocks of short texts to mine for a display or a writing magazine. Pupils may wish to redraft selected pieces, though there is a danger that this will remove the sense of spontaneity from their work.

Just one word of warning. Margaret Langdon found that the idea stopped working as soon as she prescribed a clichéd subject like 'spring'. You do need to be a little inventive about which topics you choose. Provided you are, this is a great way to teach poetry without ever mentioning that the texts the pupils are writing are in fact poems.

VERBALIZATION

The problem with getting started can be that you have to think about two things at once – what you are going to write about and how you are going to say it. You can remove this overload by providing pupils with non-verbal stimuli and asking them to verbalize them. The very existence of such stimuli in front of the pupils can give them a sense of security.

Examples of such stimuli include: photographs; pictures; objects; people; the surroundings. Sometimes simply providing these stimuli is enough. Usually, though, it helps to discuss them. This helps pupils both to notice things about the stimuli and to find words with which to describe or discuss them. Explore questions: 'What's this made out of?' 'What's this for?' 'Where did that come from?'

I learnt the power of objects from a school trip in my first year of teaching to a wonderful museum in Cambridge named Kettle's Yard. The museum, which is set in the founder's house, blends works of art with objects such as simple arrangements of pebbles. The trip produced the richest collection of pupils' writing I've ever encountered.

Simply describing objects or other stimuli can be enough, but you may wish to use them in more sophisticated ways – comparing them, say, or evaluating them or (as in Idea 53) combining them in narratives.

Children are very often happy to write lists. Lists such as 'My top ten. . .' or '20 ways to say. . .' can exert a strong fascination. Lists are so much part of our everyday culture that we almost forget that they are writing at all – which means that even pupils who are generally resistant to writing are likely to cooperate in producing them.

Lists may be valuable in their own right. They can also be useful as the starting point for more developed writing. Can you, for example, tell a story (with a beginning, middle and end) simply by listing ten words? If you've listed ten nouns, try adding an adjective (or perhaps a verb) to each line. Or write a line of description after each item in a list.

You very rapidly get to something approximating poetry. This potential can be developed further by reading some list poems, which are surprisingly popular in a great many cultures in both folk poetry ('30 days hath. . .') and high art. Get a secondhand copy of the anthology, *The Chatto Book of Cabbages and Kings*.

Lists may be the starting point for planning quite lengthy pieces (essays, debates, and so on) too.

The planning and preparation process

USING DIAGRAMS

Often the best way for pupils to plan a piece of writing is to use a diagram. Probably the most widely used is the spider diagram. You put the main topic in a circle in the middle of the page. At the end of each leg of the spider you then write a sub-topic. Each sub-topic might form a paragraph in a piece of writing. Usually it is best if you number the legs before you start the writing.

Another form of diagram is the tree diagram (like a family tree). Tree diagrams are useful when you want to base a piece of writing on a hierarchy of facts or ideas or possibly on a chronological structure. Precisely because it is hierarchical, however, this kind of diagram proves to be too restrictive for other forms of writing.

Taking-a-line-for-a-walk is a looser form of diagram. One idea leads to another. That second idea might lead to, say, three other ideas. Of those three ideas, perhaps one leads to another two ideas. Perhaps one of these ideas leads back to the first idea. And so on. Lines sprout all over the page. Sometimes taking-a-line-for-a-walk is great for generating ideas but the resulting diagram proves too complex to act as a plan for writing. In such cases, bring in a second, simpler, form of diagram.

Teach pupils how to construct diagrams by doing some together as a class. Experiment with creating conventions (for example, what do dotted lines stand for?) Play around with colour coding. Don't be surprised if your pupils are more inventive than you are. And, once they've got used to constructing diagrams as study tools, show how easily spider, tree, and taking-a-line-for-a-walk diagrams can turn into each other.

This is my all-time favourite. Simply draw a grid of nine boxes – three columns, three rows. Write a key word in each box. Even better, make that a key question. This gives you a plan for a story or project or essay or whatever. Each box becomes a paragraph or section.

You might stop there. If you want to, however, you can add a second layer of information to each box – say, an example to support the general point in each box. If pupils go on adding layers of information (perhaps colour-coded), they may find that the essay (or whatever) virtually gets written within the grid, without anyone even noticing.

You may ask what is special about the number 9. In theory, the choice of three columns and three rows is arbitrary. In practice, 3 × 3 seems to have a magical effect. Perhaps it's because it's not divisible by two – pupils basing their writing on simple binary structures (comparisons and contrasts, for example, or points for and against) always have to think of an extra idea to get to nine. Or perhaps it's because the trinitarian structure fits more complex ways of thinking – beginning, middle and end, for example, or positive, negative and interesting, or thesis, antithesis and synthesis. Whatever the reasons, it can be fun – and it seems to work.

You may forget altogether about the business of rows and columns and treat the grid as nothing more than a list of nine points. The most satisfying plans, however, come when pupils use the rows and/or columns to help pattern their thinking.

WORD BUDGETS

The funny thing about common sense is that it often isn't very common at all. Word budgets are such a simple, practical idea that you would think everybody would use them all the time. But I have found that even some experienced, published writers greet the idea as a revelation.

If a pupil has to write a piece to a specified length (300 words, say), a word budget simply requires them to allocate words to parts of their writing before they start. Give 25 words to one point, 50 words to another, and so on.

That's all there is to it. Yet – provided it is done carefully – this technique has several benefits. It helps pupils to assess, before they start writing, whether they have enough material or too much. It helps them to decide what is important.

Best of all, word budgets help to build confidence. You have to write a 900-word essay. You decide to spend 150 words on one section of it. Estimate how many paragraphs that is. Then estimate how many sentences you can fit into each paragraph. Let's say it's three. Fine. Now decide what the first sentence will be about. Write the first sentence. Now write the middle one. Now wrap it up. Bingo, you've got the paragraph done. And you can get all the other paragraphs done in the same way, adding bite-sized pieces.

A common problem for pupils when they are writing is the difficulty of thinking simultaneously about the big picture (what psychologists call the 'macrostructure') and microstructures (clauses, sentences, etc.) simultaneously. Designing a word budget helps to build a bridge between the two.

Sometimes pupils find it easier to think of questions that they wish to explore than points they wish to make. In such cases, their plans may comprise a series of questions.

Encourage pupils to generate questions using each of the following interrogatives:

○ Who? Whom?
○ What?
○ When?
○ Where? Whence? Whither?
○ Which?
○ How?
○ Why?

The advantage of including 'which?' and, especially, 'how?' and 'why?' is that it encourages pupils to write in analytical, explanatory and evaluative ways, i.e. in those ways that assessment schemes often require for the higher marks.

For some pupils and some pieces of work it may be appropriate to retain the questions in the piece of work itself, so that the pupil writes a 'Q & A' piece. In other circumstances the questions may appear only on the plan. A useful halfway house is to write a first draft in Q & A form and then to redraft into a single discursive piece.

Try taking the beginning of a newspaper article and ask pupils to see how many implicit questions are answered in the first paragraph.

HOMEWORK

Homework and writing are often uneasy bedfellows. But homework used as preparation for writing in class can be very effective indeed. In this way, homework can be used to do things that are difficult in class time – talking to members of the family or community, looking things up on the Internet or in the library.

I worked at one school where in certain year groups each pupil completed four pieces of work under exam conditions. We gave them the choice of assignments the week before. Homework was to prepare. Each pupil could bring with them notes on half a side of A4.

Some writing experts would be unimpressed by such arrangements, which were all rather regimented. But the funny thing is that it often produced good work. Twenty years later, I can still remember some of the pieces. One of the keys to success was the preparatory homework, which was achievable, purposeful, flexible and non-threatening.

Not rocket science, but it worked.

Let me introduce you to Haynes's Law. This states that children always end up doing the exact opposite of what you want them to do. Sometimes this is deliberate on their part, sometimes it is inadvertent, but the result is always the same.

The corollary of Haynes's Law is that teachers should ask pupils to do the exact opposite of what it is they really want them to do. I learnt this when I banned writing.

Helped by resources such as *The Penguin Book of Oral Poetry*, we were exploring oral cultures and the extraordinary feats of memory and creativity they sometimes performed. In order to show how much we depended on writing, I asked pupils to complete various tasks over a sequence of lessons without using writing.

Needless to say, numerous pupils cheated – to help them complete their work they started making surreptitious notes for themselves and each other. As an English teacher (i.e. as someone with responsibility for developing pupils' writing) I wasn't too upset to see this happen. I turned a blind eye. They must have thought I was pretty dumb not to notice. Then, after a few lessons, I read out a list of all the people I'd noticed 'cheating' and asked them to discuss what that showed us about writing. And this led to, yes, a piece of writing about writing.

So if you want to get pupils writing, find a way to ban it.

BANNING WRITING

Usually writing for assessment purposes needs to be in English. It doesn't follow that writing for preparatory purposes needs to be. Look back, for example, at Idea 21. If pupils had chosen to complete their notes in other languages, would it have mattered? Might it have helped? The notes were for the pupils' use only and were thrown in the bin at the end.

I remember talking to one Bengali-speaking girl. I asked her whether she ever used Bengali in school. She said that she thought it wasn't allowed.

Give your bilingual pupils the choice.

The drafting process

Pupils can be slow to grasp the opportunities of drafting. When drafting, their writing behaviour may differ little from when they are trying to write a finished piece straight off. They may think that 'drafting' is simply nothing more than an opportunity to check their spelling later.

One reason why pupils sometimes don't 'get' drafting is that they rarely see other people's rough drafts. Show them some. If you don't have any, produce some yourself.

The first rough draft I showed to a class was of a press release I'd written for the school. I photocopied it alongside the final press release that I'd sent to the newspaper. We discussed the differences between the two. In the rough draft I'd used abbreviations, crossed things out, left some gaps, and so on. As is my habit, I'd scribbled a list of ideas in the bottom right-hand corner. The whole document showed my handwriting at its worst. Without the finished copy next to it, I doubt they could have made much sense of the draft.

The important point to make is that this is all fine – I wrote the draft only for my own benefit. The final typescript, of course, needed to be complete, accurate and set out according to the conventions of a press release – that was for the newspaper's benefit.

I've also tried showing pupils copies of the drafts and jottings of professional writers, but these have made less impact. The home-made examples have always worked best.

I remember, when word processors were quite new in schools, taking a class into the computer room to write an essay. As I walked round the room I noticed that every single pupil began writing the essay at the start, i.e. with the introduction. I stopped the class for a while and pointed out that there was no need to do that – one of the beauties of word processing was that you could start anywhere and add the introduction later.

A few years later I remember taking another class into the computer room to write essays. By this time, word processors were no longer new to anyone. Guess what? The same thing happened. That technology enables different ways of writing doesn't mean that pupils will, unaided, exploit those possibilities.

The key point to explain to pupils is why it is usually best to add the introduction last. If you've already written the rest of an article or account or whatever, you know what it is that you're going to introduce. The introduction usually comes naturally. But if you don't yet know what you're introducing, it's like trying to introduce people at a party when you don't know their names.

NOT STARTING AT THE BEGINNING

WRITING FRAMES

When I first came across David Wray's work on writing frames I was deeply impressed. I felt that someone had used the kind of approach to developing pupils' writing that I was trying out, added a good deal of research-based knowledge of applied linguistics, and organized everything into a set of flexible, easy-to-use resources.

If you are not yet familiar with Wray's work, get a copy of *Writing Frames* (co-authored with Maureen Lewis) and visit his website (www.warwick.ac.uk/staff/ D.J.Wray). Wray divides pupils' writing into certain genres: recounting; reporting; explaining; procedural writing; persuasive writing; discussion. For each genre he produces worksheets consisting of boxes for pupils to fill in with their writing. Each box is introduced with some connecting text provided by Lewis and Wray ('One explanation is that. . .The evidence for this is. . .An alternative explanation is. . .') You can download copies from the website.

I remain impressed by Wray's resources. Not all teachers share my views, though I feel the critics have overlooked Wray's stipulation that 'writing frames should only be used when children have a purpose for writing'. Some argue that able writers in their class do not need writing frames. This, as Wray himself points out, is true – though sometimes teachers overlook the possibilities of themselves designing more advanced writing frames. Overall, there can be few classrooms where writing frames cannot play a major role in helping pupils to draft their work.

The single greatest advantage of seeing writing as a process is that it allows you to write badly. If, when I'm writing, it's not coming easily and I'm aware that what I'm producing is no good, I don't let it worry me. I push on regardless. Why? Because I know I can come back and revise the text. And rewriting text that you've already produced is usually a great deal easier that producing good text out of thin air.

The opportunity to redraft work not only helps pupils at the redrafting stage – it also helps them to generate text in the first place. Which is not to say that they won't need reassurance.

ANYTHING IS BETTER THAN NOTHING

AVOIDING ARBITRARY RULES

I once taught an exam class in partnership with another teacher. She told our pupils that they weren't allowed to use the word 'I' in their essays. They were somewhat perplexed – not surprisingly, since the exam board's assessment criteria called for 'personal response'. I asked her why she'd made this stipulation. She told me that when she had been a pupil her teacher had told her the same thing. I didn't hunt down her teacher to ask the reason for the rule but I suspect that, if I had, I might have been told that when s/he was a pupil. . .

My daughter, adopting the same principle, has frequently told me off for beginning sentences with words such as 'and' and 'but'. When the authors of the King James Bible wrote 'And God said, let there be light: and there was light. And God saw the light, that it was good', did a teacher pop up with a red pen and say, 'You mustn't do that!'? What do such teachers think when an English rugby crowd sings 'Jerusalem'?

I do understand the benefit of some simple, general prohibitions. Most of the Ten Commandments, for example, seem to me commonsensical. But the moralistic finger-wagging provoked by a word such as 'because' defeats me. Yes, there are occasions where the use of the word 'I' is inappropriate. And (whoops – done it again!) young children, especially, need to be encouraged to begin sentences in a variety of ways. But arbitrary rules are not the way to do it.

Arbitrary rules will not simply hamper pupils' writing (it's usually much harder, for example, to express a personal response without using the first person) but also give pupils the sense that writing is a minefield of irrationality.

Even professional authors know what it is like to experience writer's block, so it isn't surprising if pupils sometimes have the same problem.

There are in fact two types of writer's block. There are psychological blocks and there are procedural ones. The former occur when we cannot bring ourselves to write, the latter when we don't know what to write.

Psychological blocks tend to occur either when writers feel that the task is too great or that they will not measure up. The solution to the first is either to downsize the task or to help the pupil to break it into smaller components (see Idea 19 for an example). The solution to the second is to remind the pupil that there is an opportunity, through redrafting, of improving their work later – and that, in any case, something is better than nothing.

The solution to a procedural block is usually to ensure that the pupil has an adequate plan. Rather than help the pupil with the next sentence of the text, your time is better spent reworking the plan. It may help to suggest that the pupil jump to some other part of the text and come back to the difficult part later.

WRITING AS A SOLUTION TO WRITER'S BLOCK

Literature is full of examples of authors writing about not being able to write. Such oxymoronic behaviour is one of the best solutions to writer's block. Writer's block often involves a vicious circle – the best solution to a block is simply to start writing, but the block prevents the writer doing so.

If a pupil is experiencing a psychological block – see Idea 29 – advise them to write instead about all the things that they think may be preventing them from writing.

If the block is procedural, the problem may be that the pupil feels that there are too many options available. The next sentence or paragraph could go in a number of different ways and they don't know which to choose. In this case, ask them to write about *that*. Ask them to spell out what the alternatives are and what the pros and cons might be.

Usually once a writer starts writing about a block they write themselves out of it.

The redrafting process

SHARING EXAMPLES

In my experience, little of value will happen if you simply tell pupils to redraft something. Gifted writers may take the opportunity to genuinely redraft their writing. The rest will do nothing, or simply check the spelling, or waste time by just copying everything out again – though perhaps a little more neatly.

In Idea 24 I mentioned that I'd given pupils copies of both the first draft and the finished copy of a press release. As it happened, I had also kept an intermediate draft I'd written. This made it easier to discuss how I'd moved from first draft to final copy. But even without that intermediate draft we could have inferred some of the moves.

Talk about redrafting. Talk about what it is like. My favourite image is Howard Becker's description of seeing a piece of his writing after it had been copy-edited: 'I felt the way I do when, looking through the viewfinder of my camera, I give the lens that last quarter turn that brings everything into perfect focus' (*Writing for Social Scientists*, p. 79).

Talk about:

o what needs to happen when writers redraft
o the way that a change in one part of a text often requires adjustments in other parts too
o the way that texts often get shorter in the process of redrafting as writers prune their work.

Best of all, do some redrafting together. Take a very short text – perhaps just a couple of sentences from some workaday document such a letter home from school – put it on the board and see how many ways you can find to improve it.

I struggled quite a bit with finding effective ways of teaching redrafting. I eventually felt that I'd started to crack the problem when I was given the idea on a training course of teaching pupils to use symbols. (I confess I can't remember who gave me this idea, otherwise I'd gladly credit them!)

I taught pupils to put the following symbols in the margin when they read their first drafts:

↑ = Expand this bit, say more about this

↓ = Reduce this, condense it, or cut it out

↔ = Change this round a bit, make it better

👓 = Look at this carefully, it needs real attention

☺ = Like it! Good bit!

? = Eh? You what? Don't get it!

I found that pupils often liked using these symbols – especially the glasses, which were fun to draw. Using symbols is quicker than writing comments and doesn't break the concentration. There are enough symbols here to stimulate a variety of suggestions for redrafting but not too many to remember.

It is often at the redrafting stage that the focus needs to switch from the needs of the writer to the needs of the reader – see Idea 6 – so it can be beneficial for pupils to read each other's work at this stage and for the teacher, teaching assistants and so on, to get involved.

SYMBOLS FOR REDRAFTING

OTHER WAYS OF SAYING

It is when pupils are redrafting work that it is useful to introduce the concept of synonyms. In any particular assignment, there are likely to be certain words that pupils have repeated too often in their first draft. For example, in story-writing they are likely to overuse the word 'said'. It is fun to challenge the class to see how many alternatives they can generate. It makes a good homework.

It is here that it is useful to show how to use a thesaurus (and, incidentally, to insist that they learn its name so that they don't forever refer to 'that book – you know, the one with all the words in').

Of course, the first time pupils use a thesaurus there is the danger that they will go overboard and produce a piece of writing full of florid and/or inappropriate phrases. Relax, go with the flow/flux/undertow/rip tide!

Once you've established the idea of synonyms (see Idea 33) you can, with more advanced classes or pupils, explore the way that words are never perfect synonyms. Swapping a word for a so-called synonym always changes the meaning or nuance, even if only subtly.

You can have a lot of fun teaching pupils to code-switch between English derived from Northern European languages and English derived from Romance languages. Don't worry if neither you nor your pupils are very learned in etymology – it isn't necessary. Just consider, for example, the contrasting words we use to label the naughty parts of the body and the actions we perform with them.

Take a few sentences of a text and help the class to experiment with code-switching. So, to take the example of a drinking song,

Show me the way to go home.
I'm tired and I wanna go to bed.
I had a little drink about an hour ago. . .

becomes:

Indicate the way to my habitual abode.
I'm fatigued and I wish to retire.
I partook a little liquor sixty minutes ago. . .

EXPLOITING THE IMPERFECTION OF SYNONYMS

PARENTHESES

Knowing when to use parentheses is a delicate issue. You can use parentheses when some idea is relevant enough to need including but is of only minor importance. To make that judgement you need to have some sense of your text as a whole. This can be difficult when you have yet to finish the text. It is easier when you are redrafting. You might then decide that some part of what you have written needs to be subordinated – so you place it in parentheses. Or you decide that something you omitted needs to be brought in, but only in a marginal way. You add it to your text in parentheses.

The redrafting stage can be a good time to coach pupils on the mechanics of parentheses – as well as the use of brackets you can introduce dashes (*not* hyphens) and commas. For some reason, many pupils never use brackets, even though they usually understand them when they encounter them in their reading. I suspect that schools sometimes give the impression that brackets are improper, though how or why is a mystery to me.

Admittedly, the first time you teach a pupil to use brackets, it tends to produce a rash. My advice is to relax and, like lots of rashes, it will tend to go away. You're more likely to get a rash if you try teaching brackets to a whole class rather than to the individuals who need them at a particular time.

Often professional writers use redrafting as an opportunity to reduce the length of their pieces. They find more concise ways of saying things. They leave the weaker or less relevant parts out altogether.

Although this can be one of the most satisfying aspects of the writing process, it can be difficult to convince pupils of the fact. They can be very reluctant to cut. Often they are only too aware of the work that has gone into writing something in the first place and feel that if they cut something out the time has been wasted. And they might feel that they would get fewer marks for a shorter piece.

The solution is to establish an ethos based on quality. Your comments in class, the comments you write on their work, the assessment criteria you use, and – crucially – the assessment objectives you give to the pupils need to focus on quality.

Explain that omitting the weaker parts of a text raises the average quality of the writing and hence the grade it will achieve. You may add, very truthfully, that you have other things to do at home besides marking, so you don't think kindly of pupils wasting your time with texts that are longer than need be. This is a good illustration of a general point about redrafting, i.e. that at this point the needs of the reader should become paramount (see Idea 6).

Sometimes you need to set a target: 'I want you to reduce this by at least XX words.'

PLEONASMS

One of the neatest ways to show pupils how to improve texts by editing them is to sensitize them to pleonasms. These are phrases that include redundant words. For example: 'added bonus' (what kind of bonus isn't added?); 'local derby'; 'free gift'; 'forward planning'; 'never ever'; 'repeat again'; 'report back'. Often pleonasms are formed by spelling out the final term of an acronym – so 'Personal Identification Number' becomes 'PIN number', for example.

Pupils often enjoy learning the word 'pleonasm' and what it means. Teaching them to identify pleonasms can be pleasantly subversive. Such knowledge provides great opportunities for one-upmanship.

The opening of Thomas Gray's 'Elegy Written in a Country Church Yard' is one of the most famous passages of English poetry. It is also one of the most pleonastic.

> *The curfew tolls the knell of parting day,*
> *The lowing herd wind slowly o'er the lea,*
> *The ploughman homeward plods his weary way,*
> *And leaves the world to darkness and to me.*

Of course, pleonasm is not the only form of redundancy. But helping pupils to become aware of pleonasm helps to sensitize them to other kinds of laziness and sloppiness in writing.

Completing
the process

WHAT *NOT* TO DO ABOUT SPELLING

If a pupil asks you for a spelling, don't sound it out across the room, letter by letter. If you do, they might transcribe it properly on that occasion (which would show only that you know how to spell the word) but will need to ask you for the same spelling next time. Write it down for them and show them how to look at the letter strings it contains.

If a pupil makes an error by confusing two words (e.g. 'there', 'their'), teach that pupil the difference. In all other situations, do not teach confusables. If you do, the chances are that, no matter how good a teacher you are, far more pupils will end up confusing the words than was the case before you started – you will have made things worse. (See the definition of Haynes's Law in Idea 22.)

Don't use word games that consist of destroying or reversing letter sequences.

If a pupil has made numerous spelling errors, do not mark every one. You know that s/he won't learn them all.

Inculcate healthy attitudes: spelling matters; you can always improve your spelling; spelling can even be fun.

Remember to teach the spelling not only of subject-specific words (e.g. 'cell') but also general words (e.g. 'although'). Get pupils to use those words in their writing as soon as possible after you've taught them.

When pupils ask you for help with spelling, ask them to guess first. Draw attention to the parts they got right. Recognize that, because of the inconsistency of English spelling, even incorrect guesses may be intelligent.

Support spelling through your marking. Mark selectively. Reward correct spelling.

Encourage fluent handwriting. Pupils who join letters together tend to remember letter strings better.

Play word games that highlight serial probability (i.e. those that encourage pupils to think in terms of likely letter strings).

If you don't already do so, teach the look-cover-write-check method. In the first stage, teach pupils to really look at a word. For example, compare it to words that share letter strings and derivations, point out common prefixes and suffixes, show how to analyse the word in parts.

WHAT TO DO ABOUT SPELLING

PUNCTUATION IN GENERAL

Punctuation could be taught more effectively than is often the case. To do this, we need to do the following.

1 Avoid trying to teach punctuation purely through exercises. Integrate your teaching of punctuation into more general work with or about language. For example, if you're teaching pupils to use capital letters for place names, combine that with, say, some work on map skills or the origins of place names.

2 Avoid trying to teach it all in a rush. The important point, after all, is not to be able to say that you've taught something – what matters is that pupils do actually learn as a result. Allow enough time. Avoid confusing pupils or overloading their memory by trying to teach too much in the same lesson.

3 Avoid teaching about errors except when remedial action is needed. If you highlight a possible error before a pupil has made it, you will make the error more likely to occur.

4 Avoid seeing only the errors. In your marking, register signs of progress. Reward pupils when they start to get things right.

We want to avoid pupils seeing punctuation and symbolization as some sort of optional extra. Ask them to look at a keyboard. All of the keys have been put there for a purpose. Imagine the writer decided not to use some of the letters: wouldn't that be a handicap? (It is in fact fun, just as a filler, to ask pupils to write a short text without using certain letters.) Well, if writers wouldn't normally want to handicap themselves by not using some of the letters, why should they want to do so by not using some of the other keys?

There are some symbols on my keyboard that I don't understand. My keyboard has a '~'. I am ignorant of this mark: I simply do not know what it means. It is outside my knowledge. There are other marks the meaning of which I do understand (to some extent at least) but which I do not use. For example '|' and '['. My knowledge of these marks is passive. Then there are marks that I both understand and use. For example – probably rather unusually for a British person – I use '#' to mean 'number'. My knowledge of these marks is active.

Ask pupils to sort the keys in front of them into three types – those they are ignorant of, those that they have only a passive knowledge of, and those that they have an active knowledge of. Now concentrate on moving symbols up the cognitive ladder, as it were. Set some very short exercises in which pupils, preferably working collaboratively, have to use symbols that have hitherto been on the passive knowledge step of the ladder.

ACTIVATING KNOWLEDGE OF SYMBOLS

APOSTROPHE OF OMISSION

The main problem with apostrophes arises when teaching both kinds (omission and possession) at the same time. There is no earthly reason for doing so. It just confuses people. Teach the two different kinds of apostrophe on different occasions.

Work on the apostrophe of omission from both directions. Help pupils to work out (a) which letters have been omitted when they read words with apostrophes of omission and (b) which letters to leave out (and hence where the apostrophe should go) when they use the apostrophe of omission in their own writing. Set separate exercises for reading and writing.

People often get a bit worked up about apostrophes. Explain that the apostrophe of omission is a friend – a device to save time and space. Point out examples from local road signs and lane markings. Think how much wider the signs and roads would need to be without these!

You don't need to cover all types of apostrophe of omission at once. Little and often may be best. For example, a lesson on *n'ts* one week (*don't, can't*, etc.) and a lesson on terminal abbreviations (*huntin', shootin', and fishin'*) a couple of weeks later. Build into your lessons somewhere the fact that apostrophes of omission can be used with numbers too (*the '70s*).

Show how the word 'apostrophe' is spelt and teach pupils to use it. Talk of 'one of them squiggly things' belittles the apostrophe.

Teach the apostrophe of possession separately from the apostrophe of omission. It may be the same mark on the page, but it has different functions. There is no sense in confusing them.

When teaching the apostrophe of possession, include both reading and writing exercises. When reading, show how to convert phrases such as *Madonna's voice* into *the voice of Madonna*. In writing show how to change, for example, *Chelsea's manager* into *the manager of Chelsea* and vice versa.

One problem with the teaching of apostrophes is that it tends to be done only through sentence-length exercises. This makes it difficult for pupils to see why the apostrophe of possession is useful. Look at some examples in context (for example, in the text of a story) in order to show how they contribute to the economy and rhythm of writing.

For some reason, we get a bit hung up about apostrophes used with plural nouns. I suspect this happens through trying to teach everything at once. Teach pupils to hang on to the basic principles that (a) the apostrophe follows the possessor or owner and (b) you add an 's' when it sounds right. There is no need for convoluted explanations about words with a terminal 's'. I suspect that the horrible examples I see in shops (e.g. *orange's*) stem from well-intentioned teachers going on about the terminal 's'. Don't do it – stick to the principles!

Suggest that pupils look out for examples where businesses have 'cheated' by dropping the apostrophe of possession. The railway network is a particular offender, as citizens of places like Bishop's Stortford will know.

APOSTROPHE OF POSSESSION

Contrary to popular belief, the punctuation of speech is not particularly difficult. To be more precise: it is complex, because there are several different components, but no one aspect is difficult to understand.

There is no advantage whatsoever in trying to teach all aspects of the punctuation of speech at the same time. Trying to teach them all together maximizes the chances of confusion.

Fortunately the most fundamental point – learning which words go inside the speech marks – is also the easiest. Use the telephone as an illustration – explain that only those words that pass down the line need to go inside the inverted commas.

You can have some fun with simple oral, dramatic, or creative writing tasks based on telephones. It's a shame, from this point of view, that we don't seem to get crossed wires any more, but we do still get wrong numbers and hence the risk of mistaken identity, which can form the basis of a short sketch. Once you've generated some text, you can teach pupils to transcribe it using inverted commas and adding 'she said', etc.

Use too the example of comic strips. Anyone who can read them at all understands the principle of the speech bubble.

Use both reading and writing exercises. For example, ask a group of pupils to read aloud the dialogue from a short story with one of them playing the part of the narrator doing the 'he said' bits. Turn a few lines from a play script into the dialogue of a novel.

Because there are so many forms you can use (telephone, drama, oral work, play script, fiction, cartoon, etc.) you can revisit the use of inverted commas several times without making it tedious. Concentrate all the time on getting the right words inside the inverted commas.

After pupils have learnt the function of inverted commas in the punctuation of speech (Idea 44) – and it needn't be straight after – teach the paragraphing part. Explain that you drop down a line when the speaker changes.

Use both reading and writing. Show in the dialogue of a short story how helpful the paragraphing is in signalling a change of speaker. Ask pupils to transcribe a conversation (for example, taken from a play script, a comic strip or a piece of class drama) into prose dialogue.

Ensure that pupils very soon have the opportunity to incorporate the principle into an authentic, sustained, piece of writing (i.e. not an exercise). Refuse to check it until pupils have checked the paragraphing. Ask them to press the return key or (on paper) insert an oblique ('/') in red wherever they have forgotten to signal a new paragraph.

Teaching pupils to paragraph speech makes their work clearer and more spacious. This makes it easier then to teach – though, again, not necessarily straightaway – capitalization and the insertion of commas and stops before, within, and after inverted commas. Again, there is no point in teaching all these at once. The insertion of a comma before the opening of inverted commas is relatively easy to teach, so why complicate it with all the other stuff at the same time?

BEYOND INVERTED COMMAS

Often the results of asking pupils to check their work are disappointing. Merely saying 'Check your work' makes little impact. But there are ways of putting this right.

The worst time for checking is usually straight after the pupil has finished writing. Create some distance. For example, give the piece of work back at the beginning of the next lesson. Ask students, before they start checking, to look back through their previous work. What are their characteristic errors? What targets for improvement have they been given? Use these to inform their checking.

Inculcate the right attitude. Explain to pupils that if they're convinced that there are no errors, they probably won't find any – but if they tell themselves there *are* errors and it's their job to find them, they probably will.

Give examples of when you've been pleased you've checked something. I've lost count of how many times I've told the story of my German exam. I knew I was a borderline pass/fail. I finished the exam over half an hour early. I spent all the rest of the time systematically checking – firstly cases, then noun/adjective agreement, then tenses, and so on. I scraped a pass. Such stories do seem to have some effect on pupils.

Teach pupils to focus on particular sources of error. For example, ask pupils who have just written a story to focus on the passages of dialogue and check that they have begun each new speech on a new line. This is often more productive than asking pupils to check everything at once.

Train pupils to work in pairs to check their work together or to check each other's. Try checking spelling by reading from the bottom line up.

The presentation and publishing stage of writing provides a good opportunity for learning about such matters as handwriting, text design, illustration and reading aloud.

Establish a bank of text designs consisting both of examples of pupils' work and professional texts. Pupils can help you to collect all kinds of ephemera – leaflets, tickets, letters, packaging – that may provide presentational ideas.

If, like me, you have not had a visual training, I recommend that you obtain a copy of *The Non-designer's Design Book*. Although written for adults, much of it is usable with children.

Teach that good design is about appropriateness. The best design might not be, for example the most colourful. Presentation involves questions of meaning, audience and appropriateness.

Although it won't make me popular, I appeal to you to avoid the old puritanism (the school needs to save money on paper) and the new puritanism (giving pupils plenty of paper is bad for the environment). If presentation of work requires plentiful supplies of paper, then so be it. We can afford it, really.

Keith Topping, a psychologist at Dundee University, has pioneered a scheme of paired writing whereby a pupil works with either a more skilled pupil or an adult in order to produce some written work collaboratively. Though the basic idea is far from new, Topping's methods help to organize the process and provide a new level of rigour. I will outline them here – the detail is explained in his book, *Thinking Reading Writing*.

Topping suggests that pairs working on a piece of writing together proceed through six stages:

1 Ideas generation and mapping
2 Drafting
3 Reading the draft
4 Editing the draft together
5 Producing a best copy
6 Evaluation.

For each stage Topping has produced detailed resources to support the pairs and guide their progress. For example, he provides ten questions to help generate ideas in stage 1. The resources are available on the University of Dundee website (www.dundee.ac.uk/ fedsoc/research/projects/trwresources/writing).

For stage 4 Topping suggests that pairs edit drafts on four levels, namely meaning (NB wording), order (NB grammar), spelling (including capitalization), and punctuation. A more advanced edit may include issues such as the focus, quality of ideas and purpose.

Obviously one can use paired work for development without following Topping's precise structure or his materials. They do, however, have the advantage of making everyone clear about what they should be doing when. They provide a sense of security.

Tasks

A QUESTION OF PURPOSE

There is no shortage of writing tasks available for teachers to set. You can get them off the peg, particularly from ELT sites. Just try a little gentle Googling.

The problem is not finding tasks, but working out why anyone would want to do the ones you find. The majority of tasks I have just Googled are either presented free of any purpose or related only to teacherly purposes. For example, one assignment I've just found on www.onestopenglish.com is offered in order 'To help students produce writing with a higher occurrence of lexical variation, complex sentences and appropriate use of passive structures.' This might be a very good reason to set work – I don't want to dismiss it – but it might not fully assuage the kids in our classrooms who ask, 'Why do we have to do this?'

People tend to write best when they have a purpose. We write, for example, in order to: accuse; advertise; alert; agree; amuse; apologize; appeal; apply; announce; appraise; arrange; articulate; ask; assert; bemoan; bequeath; bid; blackmail; cancel; celebrate; challenge; check; claim; clarify; comfort; commend; communicate; complain; conceal; confirm; confuse; consider; convince; correct; criticize; decide; declare; define; defraud; describe; disagree; discourage; dissent; emote; encourage; enable; enlighten; enquire; entertain; evoke; exclaim; excuse; explain; explore; expose; express; familiarize; guide; illustrate; impress; influence; inform; instruct; joke; judge; market; mislead; narrate; negotiate; note; notify; obfuscate; order; persuade; pitch; placate; postpone; predict; prevent; protest; query; quiz; quote; rage; rant; rebut; record; recount; refuse; remind; renege; request; report; reveal; schedule; seduce; sell; share; teach; tell; think; threaten; trade; train; urge; or warn.

Use the above list to ensure that your pupils learn to use writing for a range of purposes. Avoid restricting their writing to the usual school diet – i.e. lots of explaining, describing, narrating, and persuading, not so much challenging, dissenting, protesting, or refusing!

Below is an A–Z (well, almost!) of genres or forms that you may ask pupils to write in. The list provides plenty of options for short, medium, and long pieces of writing. Use it to extend pupils' experience of writing beyond the forms in which they are most commonly asked to write at school. Here's the list:

abstract; acrostic; advertisement; anagrams; anecdote; announcement; aphorism; appeal; application; article; autobiography; ballad; biography; bibliography; blog; blurb; brief; bulletin; cameo; caption; case study; code; commentary; competition; complaint; confession; congratulations; contract; critique; curse; CV; description; diagnosis; diary; dictionary; directions; editorial; elegy; email; episode; epistle; essay; fact file; fable; fairy story; flyer; footnotes; forecast; foreword; game; glossary; greetings card; guide; haiku; headline; horoscope; hymn; index; interview; introduction; instructions; invitation; invoice; itinerary; joke; journal; kenning; lament; leaflet; lecture; letter; limerick; listing; log; lonely hearts page; lyric; manifesto; manual; memo; memoir; menu; monologue; motto; newsletter; notes; notice; nursery rhyme; obituary; order; parody; pastiche; plan; poem; petition; portrait; postcard; prayer; preface; problem page; profile; prognosis; programme; prophecy; proposal; protocol; proverb; Q & A; quiz; rap; receipt; recipe; recommendation; record; reference; reply; report; review; riddle; rule; schedule; scorecard; script; sequel; sermon; sketch; slogan; song; sound bite; specification; speech; spell; strapline; statement; story; summary; survey; table; template; tender; test; text message; tips; translation; travelogue; eulogy; valentine; web page; will; X-word; exam; A–Z.

DEFINING THE AUDIENCE

I said in Idea 7 that we need to specify the audience when setting an assignment. Here is a list to choose from to help you do just that. In some cases pupils will be writing for the audience *in actual fact*, in others they will be writing *as if* for the audience.

Personal audiences:

o The pupil him/herself
o Other pupils in the class
o You, the teacher
o Pupils in other classes
o Other teachers
o Other people in the school
o Pupils of other schools
o Penfriends
o Members of the pupil's family
o Members of the local community
o Editors
o Business people
o Public figures
o Characters from books or other texts
o Historical figures.

Impersonal audiences:

o People of a particular age
o People living in a particular area
o People with a particular interest or level of expertise
o Unspecified.

At one point in *Writing* – one of the best books on the subject I've read – novelist George V. Higgins considers three narratives – an article by Gay Talese about baseball legend Joe DiMaggio, a memoir of the Pacific War by William Manchester, and a story by Irwin Shaw set in New York.

The texts are, in many ways, very different from each other, but Higgins draws attention to a similarity in the way they begin, namely what he calls 'the oblique approach they take to a subject that none [of the authors] ever states directly. In each instance, the writer takes good care to situate his reader in the context of his protagonist, and allows – indeed, requires – the reader to deduce from the data provided what has happened to his hero that merits narration of his story. You know at once where you are, and who is your companion, and why you should be interested in what happens to him. That is entirely good enough.' Reading, Higgins argues is a 'participatory sport', which means that you should 'never tell your reader what your story is about'.

Provide pupils with examples of narratives – preferably a mixture of fiction and non-fiction – in which the openings work in the way that Higgins identifies. You won't find such narratives hard to find – many of the narratives you already teach with will work. Discuss the openings with questions derived from Higgins's account. Do you know who the protagonist is? Can you infer from the clues provided what has happened that merits attention? Then ask pupils each to write one such opening – without actually telling the reader what their stories are about.

I've had both school pupils and adult students produce some excellent coursework based on this idea. See whether pupils can guess from reading each other's openings what their stories are really about.

THE STORY OF THREE OBJECTS

This is a corny idea. It was around when I was a lad and probably for long time before that. The idea is simply to write a story containing three objects. It doesn't much matter what the objects are – a ladder, a bar of soap, a brick, a compass, a glass, a ring, a piece of rope, whatever. Just make sure that you, rather than the writer, specify the objects – it's more likely to stretch the imagination that way.

I guess the task works because it encourages pupils to plan ahead and also to think episodically – often one object provides the opening, one the middle, and one the ending. The only stipulation you need to make – and often it isn't necessary – is that the writer should actually *use* the objects in the plot, rather than just mention them.

That's it. Teaching isn't always simple but on this occasion it is.

In *Wild Mind* Natalie Goldberg writes about a novel she is writing: 'In chapter twenty, I know Nell begins in Boulder and is driving to Nebraska. I know at the end of the chapter she has to be in the town of Norfolk. . .I say to myself, "Okay, go for an hour," or longer. I don't know what will happen in those miles of driving. I only find out while I write' (p. 60).

Her point is that often it doesn't do to plan – often the thinking develops through the writing – a point I am sympathetic to. When it comes to teaching, however, pupils sometimes need more support than that. 'Creative writing' got a bad name in schools because too often pupils set off on hour-long journeys with no clear idea where they were going. Their stories foundered and they learnt little.

Try turning Goldberg's idea round. Instead of writing without a plan, plan without writing. Give pupils two situations, one for the beginning of a chapter and one for the end, and ask them to devise plots for getting from one to the other. They can present them to each other. If pupils come up with really good ideas, they may if they want to then write the chapter – but I wouldn't make them do it just for the sake of it.

You can use this lesson in a free-floating way or as a warm-up exercise for a narrative the pupils are going to read. If used in the latter way, it helps the pupils to focus, when you read the actual chapter, on *how* the author has constructed the story.

DESIGNING PLOTS

55

Pupils often gain a sense of pride from completing a sustained piece of writing, but can feel daunted beforehand. You can help by 'chunking' long tasks into a series of shorter ones.

Telling a story through an exchange of letters between characters, rather than through a narrator, has a long pedigree in English literature. It dates back to eighteenth-century novelists such as Tobias Smollett. In our own time the tradition has been rejuvenated in the form of stories constructed out of exchanges of email.

Experience suggests that seven is the magic number. Seven letters (or emails, postcards, or whatever) allows enough space for a story of some weight and complexity to develop without tedium setting in. Use two characters or three. That seven is indivisible by either two or three seems to me somehow to be another reason why it works.

Between letters you can gradually teach pupils more about how the form works. You can explain, for example, how characters may withhold or distort the truth and how readers might find themselves in a privileged position of seeing though a character or knowing more than one of the characters does.

Able pupils may plan an entire story before writing the first letter, but with most pupils it's better just to get started. Ideas will come as they write and as you drop in suggestions ('Now bring in a third letter-writer') between letters. Emphasize that pupils may always go back and revise earlier letters to make them fit better with an emerging idea.

You can play with this form, asking pupils to predict each other's next letters or to collaborate in pairs.

This is one of my favourites. Pupils write their autobiographies as if they have grown old. I've always used a four-chapter structure, but I guess that isn't sacrosanct.

The pupils imagine that they are, say, 80. The first chapter tells the story of their youth, finishing a few years later than they actually are now. The second takes them up to 30 or so. The third is middle age and the fourth is old age.

It's a marvellous way of considering numerous rites of passage – first dates, getting a job, getting a car, leaving home, setting up a home of one's own, getting married, travelling, being made redundant, becoming a parent, getting divorced, getting promoted, falling ill, achieving ambitions, retiring, whatever.

You can bring in all kinds of stimuli – poetry, passages from fiction and play scripts, non-fiction, photographs, interviews, certificates, trophies, maps, you name it. And you don't need to do it all yourself, since pupils can gather materials for homework. There is a great opportunity to look at realia – what do the words of various wedding ceremonies actually say, for example?

One technique I've always built in is visioning. Think of yourself at a certain age in the future. Don't just think of yourself, see yourself. Form one precise image of yourself as you imagine yourself at that time. Hold that image. Fill it out. Now describe it – in detail. Where are you? What posture are you adopting? What expression is on your face? What are you wearing? What are you doing? What's behind you? Who are you with? And so on. Now consider each detail. What does it suggest about who you are or what you want? Now get that into your writing.

WORK EXPERIENCE

Schools often do draw on pupils' experience (whether part-time work or the school's work experience programme) for written work. There is a danger, however, that such writing is limited to unambitious, if respectable, forms of writing – diary entries, responses to structured questions, and so on. Such work can be valuable, but we should remember that there are opportunities for other forms of writing.

Though canonical English literature has, I think, tended to neglect the world of work, community writing and oral histories (such as Ronald Blythe's *Akenfield* and Mary Chamberlain's *Fenwomen*) frequently contain rich accounts. If, as is likely, you don't have copies of such writing for the pupils to read themselves, this is a great opportunity for aural comprehension.

Before reading an account aloud, give pupils some questions to bear in mind as they're listening. Read the account, discuss the questions, then read at least some of the account again to bring out the effects of those features you have discussed.

My favourite is George Orwell's account of sweated labour in a 'cafeterie' in *Down and Out in Paris and London*. Read, for example, Chapter 11. Set questions that draw attention to such features as Orwell's delineation of space, sequencing of information and recording of time, listing of tasks, use of the senses, description of people, and use of telling detail. Then ask pupils to use such headings to organize accounts of their experience of work.

ON ARGUMENT

There is often a great discrepancy between pupils' ability to argue orally and their ability to compose arguments on paper. They can be all too good at the former and disappointing at the latter.

There is a reason for this, which is that oral argument, oddly enough, depends on (admittedly not very orderly) turn-taking. In oral arguments one usually talks in short passages and the cue for each new contribution often comes from something your interlocutor has just said. In written arguments, such as essays, it's often the other way round – we often want pupils to sustain and develop a single argument.

As teachers we often explain that when we say we want pupils to write an argument, we don't mean 'argument' in the sense of 'quarrel', 'row' or 'squabble'. But as soon as we do that, we break the link between the type of argument that pupils know a great deal about and the type we want them to learn – at which point all of their (genuine, if unarticulated) knowledge goes out of the window.

Build on, rather than dismiss, your pupils' knowledge of rows, quarrels, etc. Plan sequences of tasks that help your pupils to move from those types of argument to more composed, sustained, or academic forms. Ideas 59–65, for example, were designed originally as one such (loose) sequence of lessons.

Introduce the language of argument (using 'argument' in the widest sense). How do dictionaries define 'argue' and 'argument'? With the help of a thesaurus, generate some synonyms. Which languages do such words come from? What shades of meaning do these (so-called) synonyms have? Explore these words diagrammatically: produce a verbal map with the word 'argument' in the middle and words clustered together on different parts of the board.

Discuss adverbs and connectives – terms such as: 'also'; 'although'; 'and'; 'assuming'; 'because'; 'but'; 'despite'; 'even'; 'frankly'; 'furthermore'; 'honestly'; 'however'; 'if'; 'just'; 'look'; 'moreover'; 'nevertheless'; 'on the other hand'; 'perhaps'; 'quite'; 'rightly or wrongly'; 'still'; 'surely'; 'therefore'; 'unfortunately'; and 'yet'. Sift them. Which words do pupils not understand? Which words do they understand but not use? Which words would they use in speech and which in writing?

Think of labels for parts of arguments, from basic words such as 'point' and 'question', through intermediate ones like 'claim', 'issue', 'statement', and 'decision', to more sophisticated words like 'assumption', 'conclusion', 'crux', 'hypothesis', 'assertion' or 'solution'.

Having explored the vocabulary of argument, you can draw on it at each subsequent stage. Each time you do so you will help pupils first to understand and then to employ a wider range of vocabulary.

Start arguing. Here's a simple piece of drama. Work in pairs. You're siblings. Argue. Resolve the argument. Now work in fours. Two of you are children, two of you are adults. You live in the same home. The two generations argue with each other, then resolve their argument. Now work in eights. Each four is a household. The two households argue with each other, then resolve their argument. Now go for the nuclear option. Half the class live on one side of the street, half the class live on the other. . .

Afterwards there are two ways in which you can use the drama to help develop pupils' writing. First, discuss the language of argument. For example: the use of sounds that aren't quite words ('Pah!', 'Ugh?'); the way that one party seizes on (and perhaps twists) words or expressions that the other party has used; and the different role and effects of talking in the first, second, or third person. You can also discuss the role of supra-segmentals (without having to use the word) – the use of breath, pace, intonation and volume.

Now you can use this language awareness to help convert the drama into a script. I don't mean that pupils should transcribe what they've said – that would be tedious. I mean they should select some part of the drama and shape it. Turn it into a sketch – comic if you like. Give it a definite ending.

The piece is probably best written in two stages – a draft for performance and then a polished version. In between the two you can teach the class about transcription devices, for example, the use of capital letters to denote shouting, the use of brackets to separate thoughts or actions from speech, the use of italics for stress, and of ellipses for pauses.

USING DRAMA IN ARGUMENT

IDEA 61

STAGING A TRIAL

One form that helps to bridge the gap for pupils between oral and written argument is the courtroom trial. It can be fun enacting a trial in class. When I've done this I've usually found I have some pupils in my class who are, through personal experience, well equipped to advise on courtroom procedures.

For the subject matter you can often use a piece of literature that you are already studying. Note that here you do not strictly need to stick to legal issues. You could try a character for behaving unethically rather than illegally. The drama that results can be subtler.

You can also base a trial on a simple game. Tell two suspects that they will be tried for a crime committed between two precise times last weekend. Give them time in private to construct an alibi together. Then have the prosecutor – usually aided, whether you plan it that way or not, by the rest of the class – try to find a flaw in the alibi.

It may well be that in preparing for the trial pupils write notes. If so, they are in effect beginning to draft a piece of argumentative writing. After the trial you may ask pupils to write a script. More rewarding is to ask them to write an ideal speech from the point of view of either the prosecution or the defence – or both.

Choose a live political issue – I suggest one that has several different aspects and is clearly related to ethical questions. Appoint three teams – the governing party, the opposing party, and a minority party. You are the speaker. The government's job is to propose some new legislation. Ensure that the various roles – leaders, front-bench ministers, backbenchers – are allocated. You probably need to appoint yourself Speaker.

Introduce pupils, preferably through some recordings, to the main conventions of parliamentary debate – for example, that MPs address the Speaker rather than each other, that an MP wishing to speak must stand up and wait for the person speaking to give way, that MPs must avoid unparliamentary language such as 'liar'. It is not necessary to be too pinickety – this is not an old-fashioned lesson in British Constitution – but set some ground rules that establish the tone. Parliament's website (www.parliament.uk) is invaluable – see especially 'Hansard', 'How Parliament Works', 'Parliament Live', and 'Glossary'.

Give pupils a chance to compose their speeches, but explain that speeches must not be read. Suggest that leaders may make three points in their main speech, front-bench speakers two, and backbenchers one. Allow teams to meet to plan in secret. Then pull the desks back, set the chairs out appropriately and off you go.

Afterwards the debate may be converted into writing. Pupils may either write up one or more speeches for Hansard or compose a report for the media. They will want to polish what was said – which is what happens in Hansard anyway. The advantages of this simulation are that it provides a natural opportunity for redrafting and a way of building extended arguments out of shorter pieces.

PARLIAMENT

You need a motion ('This house. . .'). One person proposes the motion. Then someone opposes it. They are followed by a second proposer and a second opposer. Then there are speeches from the floor. These are followed by concluding speeches from a proposer and then from an opposer. Finally comes the vote.

Pupils write notes beforehand and may plan without being overheard by their opponents. Suggest that the first speaker on each side should cover lots of ground, making several points briefly, and that the second speaker on either side chooses one point to explore in detail. Speeches may not be read. Show pupils how to make prompt notes consisting of key words on cards.

Explain that politeness needs to ensue from the outset ('Ladies and gentlemen. . .'). You might call anyone to speak from the floor, though you'd prefer volunteers. Get yourself an effective gavel.

Afterwards pupils may write: one speech; a sequence of speeches for one side or the other; speeches on both sides; an essay in favour of one side or the other; or an essay examining both sides of the argument.

I've seen good debates on a whole variety of issues, including drugs legislation, the age of consent, and hunting. It is best if the motion is reasonably specific but able to be related to general issues. In my experience debates about school life tend not to work so well – they make the formal structure feel artificially elevated and strained.

Pupils benefit as writers of argument from practice in moving between summaries and developed arguments. They may do so in both directions – by, for example, first writing notes and then writing an essay or, on the other hand, by taking a published argument and reducing it to a condensed version.

Some readers will be able to remember the old-fashioned précis-type question that featured in examinations such as English Language O-level. Pupils would be required to write a summary of an argument in a certain number of words – let's say reducing a text from 150 words to 30–40. Such exercises tended to be pretty arid, with neither purpose nor audience specified.

It's not difficult to think of simulated forms of summary. You have to reduce a press release to a certain number of words to fit the available slot in a newsletter, for example, or find a way of presenting information in a limited space on an application form. Simulated exercises are certainly preferable to decontextualized précis.

While teaching précis, however, I did learn from colleagues two techniques that proved transferable. First, when pupils are writing a summary it is best, after they have read the original text a few times, to cover it up before they start writing in rough. Second, and more important, it is better by far to specify an exact number of words rather than a range – 36 words, say, rather than 30–40. This sounds – and is – completely arbitrary, but it has the effect of making pupils focus much more closely on such issues as phraseology, redundancy and syntax.

I simply cannot imagine why we do so little explicit teaching of logic in schools. Every subject would benefit from children learning to think more logically and yet every subject teacher leaves logic for someone else to do.

Let us consider an example. You may be old enough to remember Crosby, Stills, Nash and Young. This was a 'supergroup' formed by bringing together four very talented musicians. I've put 'supergroup' in inverted commas because they weren't super at all. It is commonly agreed that the work that each member produced individually was better than the work they produced together. This points us towards the logic of composition: what is true of each component of a group may not be true of the group as a whole.

Teaching logic would benefit pupils' writing in general but most particularly their writing of arguments. Get hold of a copy of Madsen Pirie's *How to Win Every Argument*. The logic of composition is one of over 70 arguments that Pirie explains (and illustrates) simply, concisely and wittily.

The attraction of using Pirie's book to teach from is that he recommends learning not only how to spot logical fallacies but also how to perpetrate them on others deliberately. One might not want to encourage this in pupils' coursework (!), but it has an obvious application in simulated forms of argument (see Ideas 61–63).

Teaching logic the Pirie way also has the advantage of annoying and subverting everyone else in town, from the headteacher down.

By no means all pupils get to go on holiday. But many do. And even those who don't might have the chance of going on school trips. When they do go away, they probably don't think of themselves as travel writers. Indeed, they may not even know that there is such as thing as travel writing. Yet travel writing, thanks to writers such as Bill Bryson, has become an extraordinarily popular – and accessible – form of writing.

Though they may not think of themselves as authors, your pupils might well have written postcards, or read them – or at least considered themselves capable of writing them. In *Teaching Literacy* Fred Sedgwick points out the close similarity in style between typical postcards and published travel writing.

Sedgwick's observation that the text of postcards may often, with a few judiciously inserted line breaks, be converted into passable poetry is, though intriguing, something of a distraction. More to the point is his suggestion that pupils may produce effective passages of travel writing by employing two simple stylistic devices.

First, they should use the present tense. As a reader I know I engaged with J.M. Synge's classic, *The Aran Islands*, as soon as I read the opening sentence: 'I am in Aranmor, sitting over a turf fire, listening to a murmur of Gaelic that is rising from a little public house under my room.' Second, they should employ in their descriptions all five senses. Start with unintimidating postcard-length texts that can then be redrafted into something more ambitious.

One oft-used task in schools is to write directions to enable a stranger to get somewhere, for example, the railway station. Though not a bad task, it lacks one of the attractions of the best instructional tasks i.e. the ability to test the instructions by trying them out there and then.

To test instructions in this way you need to ensure that whoever is following the instructions does not know already how to perform the activity, otherwise they will automatically fill in gaps and remove ambiguities from the instructions they have been given.

Give pupils pictures. Ask each pupil to write instructions so that someone who hasn't seen his or her picture can draw it. Then test it out and see how accurate the resulting drawings are. After a few examples, discuss the typical weaknesses of instructional writing and the features that make for success. Rerun the task in the light of these points.

The key point is for pupils to learn to switch from the writer's perspective to the reader's (see Idea 6). Once you've established that principle you can progress to less immediately testable tasks – writing recipes, for example, or instructions on how to do those things with pieces of technology (phones, computers, DVD players) that children seem to learn by osmosis and adults habitually find perplexing.

Pupils must get very tired of being told to 'write a newspaper article on. . .' How many times do they receive this instruction over the course of their time in school? Have we got a journalistic obsession? How often do pupils actually read newspaper articles? And how much do we teach them about newspapers? Often pupils' texts resemble news stories only in having a headline in large font.

If we are going to use news reporting as a medium, let's do it properly. Research suggests that, whether they know it or not, editors assess newsworthiness according to the following criteria:

○ Timeliness
○ Size: how big is the story?
○ Unusualness ('Man Bites Dog')
○ Perceived relevance to the audience
○ Dramatic value (How shocking? How unexpected? How much has changed?)
○ Lack of ambiguity: is the story simple and clear?
○ Negativity: bad news is usually 'better' than good
○ Continuity: has the story been covered before?
○ Composition: does the story help to provide the newspaper with the overall balance of subjects required?

Use these criteria to assess whether you should be setting the task as a news story in the first place. If so, teach the pupils to bring out the news value in their stories as defined by these criteria.

REPORTING THE NEWS

ANALOGIES

Compare two objects or ideas, A and B. If A resembles B in one respect, it may resemble it in other respects. Logically, there is no reason why it should. In practice, it's often worth exploring.

English literature is full of extended metaphors. Consider, for example, such metaphors in social and political thinking as (a) our society likened to a human body, (b) a government or institution seen as a mechanical contraption or (c) the comparison of life to a piece of theatre (with typical roles, stock characters, disguises, tragic or comic story-lines, and so on).

The attraction of analogical thinking is that it often enables pupils to explore one thing in terms of something already very familiar to them. In this way they can develop quite sophisticated understandings of new material in an entertaining way.

Start with something local. I remember, for example, asking pupils to compare their school to a human body. One of them pointed out, with some truth, that both tended to get smellier the lower you got.

Developing extended metaphors lends itself to work in various stages, from individual or pair work through small group work to whole class discussion. Maybe I'm just not very imaginative at this kind of thing, but I've often found pupils to be more ingenious than I am. In discussion, ingenuity can be infectious. I know of no better method for generating extended writing than asking pupils to explain and develop extended metaphors that have been worked out together on the board.

Schools are sometimes criticized for neglecting business in general and small business in particular. Here's an opportunity to do something about it. Writing a business plan might sound rather daunting, but in fact most plans for new businesses grow out of answers to simply expressed questions such as the following:

1 The basic idea: what goods or services are you going to sell?
2 Marketing and sales: who is going to buy your products? Why will they buy them? How will customers benefit from your products? How will you reach the customers? What competition is there? What will be different about what you offer?
3 Staffing: how many staff will you need and in what roles? What skills do they need? How will you go about recruitment?
4 Operations: where will your business be located? What facilities and equipment will you need?

I've omitted questions about the financial forecasts, which are probably impossible without specialist teaching.

The idea is definitely not solely for senior pupils. The scenario I've used most often is a deliberately wacky one, namely setting up a non-alcoholic pub. The idea encourages lateral thinking – how to appeal to drivers, families, the health-conscious, teetotal communities, etc.

Teams of pupils present their proposals to some potential investors, who have to decide which proposal(s) to support.

If , by the way, you'd like more information on business plans, I recommend Business Link (www.businesslink.gov.uk). Select 'Starting up', then 'Considering starting up?'

REVIEWING AND EVALUATING WEBSITES

Write a review of a website. Here are some major questions to use as prompts: Where does the website come from? What's it about? What does it cover? What's the point of it? Who is it for? What kinds of things do you learn? How easy is it to use? How attractive is it? How does it compare to other sites? How reliable or trustworthy is it?

A major task facing educators is to teach pupils why and how to evaluate websites. Whereas most of the above questions are intended as optional, I would insist on a consideration of reliability and trustworthiness. For example:

○ does the website say when information was last updated?
○ is it clear who is behind the website? Is there a terrestrial address?
○ who are the stakeholders and what interests are at stake?
○ who, if anyone, verifies, endorses, or accredits the information?
○ how could you test the accuracy of information?

Johns Hopkins University's web page 'Evaluating Information Found on the Internet' (www.library.jhu. edu/researchhelp/general/evaluating/index.html) is useful for teacher development, while the Internet Detective (www.vts.intute.ac.uk/detective/index.html) is a little more accessible for pupils.

Reviewing websites can be a useful activity in its own right, but is most valuable when taught as part of a sequence of lessons in which pupils also plan or design websites (see Ideas 72 and 73).

You don't need computer equipment available for pupils to design their own sites – you can use paper. (I've designed two websites and in each case I began with pencil and paper). Large sheets of paper (A3) are preferable. They allow space for pupils to play around with outlines for, and links between, several pages.

A decision needs to be made early on about navigation. The main form of navigation can be:

○ sequential (where the page acts merely as a scroll that one moves down either continuously or in a series of jumps);
○ hierarchical (where options that you click on take you first to general information – e.g. 'Contact us' – and then to more specific information – e.g. 'Contact our sales department';
○ associative (where links take you from one page to another but not via any hierarchical order).

Pupils also need to consider what use to make of multimedia features such as sound and video clips (and how integral these will be to the site) and of interactive features.

Website design provides opportunities for collaborative work – as often happens in the world outside school. Teams of pupils may each present their plans as if a sponsor has invited proposals for a website to fulfil a particular purpose. If pupils have already written reviews of websites (see Idea 71), they could then plan a website for Internet reviews.

PLANNING A WEBSITE

This idea is best used with Idea 72. Either design a page for a website or redesign an existing web page in order to improve it. Consider the following:

1 Alignment. Consider how you organize blocks of text and other objects both horizontally and vertically. How clear are the lines? Where should you use left-alignment and where right? Consider how to balance objects on the page.

2 Gaps and spaces. Develop conventions by deciding how closely images should be related to captions and/or accompanying text, how close headings should be to the text they relate to, and how much space should be used to separate different sections of text.

3 Contrasts. The use of contrast can help the reader to scan the page and also introduce visual interest and even surprise. Consider contrasts in colour, shape and font. What opportunities are there for colour-coding?

4 Repetition. Consider how the repetition of elements such as logos, symbols and typefaces can help to integrate a page and provide it with an overall look or style.

Writing poetry for the Internet involves – or may involve – far more than merely writing a poem and then posting it on a website. Consider also the potential for visual and multimedia effects.

Look, for example, at the work of Catherine Byron. One of her publishers – Salmon Books – has posted the text of one her poems ('Writing on skin') on their site (www.salmonpoetry.com/vellum.html). That is conventional enough – though they have also included recordings of the poet reading this and two other poems.

Byron herself has experimented with using voices as an integral part of her poetry – see, for example, 'Creel of voices' on her website (www.catherinebyron.com). She has also attended to the visual presentation of her work. She has collaborated with calligrapher Denis Brown – see his 'Quillskill' website (www.quillskill.com).

Her most interesting web poetry has been produced in collaboration with artist Eileen Coxon. To see how she has integrated text with prints and sketches, look at 'Renderers' on Byron's website. She explains some of her thinking about the writing of this poem in a journal (also accessible via the site).

Writing for the Internet has encouraged Byron to make her poems shorter and – as you see from 'Renderers' – to experiment with spacing words across the page so that you no longer read purely from left to right. She also uses layers of text to create an impression of depth.

As with Ideas 72 and 73, you do not necessarily need computer equipment for pupils to experiment with web poetry. Have them use blank paper to experiment with short works integrating words and images. These may be accompanied by live or recorded readings.

WEB POETRY

There's a lot of book reviewing going on in schools. Which is fine, except that many of the reviews that result don't read much like reviews as the term is understood outside schools.

There are two reasons for this, both of them related to the way that we tend to play rather fast and loose in school with journalistic forms of writing. First, 'reviews' are often produced in a highly structured way in response to sequences of questions provided by the teacher ('Write a paragraph outlining the plot. . . Write a paragraph about the main character'). When I worked as a reviewer for a magazine for a few years, it never occurred to me to approach the job at all like that. In fact, one of the aspects I most enjoyed was the flexibility of the form. The point of such questions is often a teacherly, rather than literary, one – it is to ensure that the pupil meets certain assessment objectives. Why, then, not just set a good ol' fashioned series of questions without confusing the issue by dressing the answers up as 'reviews'?

Second, many pupils lack models for their reviews because they often don't actually read many published reviews. Reviews are readily available on the Internet, including newspaper websites. My favourite is the *Morning Star* website (www.morningstaronline.co.uk), which includes frequent reviews of poetry and crime fiction as well as serious non-fiction. The menu on Bookweb's homepage (www.bookweb.co.uk) offers links to book review sites, including reviews of children's books and reviews by children. Reading a series of reviews – including, ideally, contrasting reviews of the same book – acquaints pupils with the language, structures, and diversity of reviewing.

I started thinking about this when I noticed that in one school I worked in boys' results in English tended not to be as good as girls'. With a colleague I started looking into why this was so. We noticed that, when it came to writing about texts, boys often showed a strong interest in plot. Many boys' default option when it came to writing about texts was simply to write out the plot – a form of writing, according to the assessment objectives that we had to apply, that could not be rewarded with a high grade.

What to do? One solution was to try to move pupils beyond recounting the plot into other forms of study, for example, character analysis. That would be fine, but we were already trying to do that.

Another solution was to accept the interest in plot and build on it. Some of us in our own literary training rather missed out on narratology and majored in character, theme and symbol instead. The danger is that as a result we tend to devalue plot.

Let's write about plot well. If we're going to summarize the plot, let's get beyond the blow-by-blow accounts. Help pupils to be selective. Try specifying the *exact* number of words. Limit the number of points – what were the six main events?

Use stepped questions. Start with a summary – it helps them to get the story straight and out of their system. Move on to analysis – what was predictable, what was unexpected? Draw a graph showing the rise and fall of tension. Introduce comparison – which stories does this one most resemble, how do they differ? Ask for an evaluation. How many stars? Why not more, why not fewer? Finish, perhaps, with creativity: write in XX words a new plot, either for a sequel or a book in the same series/genre.

WRITING ABOUT PLOT

IMITATION

This is an idea that I have borrowed and adapted from Dorothea Brande's classic guide, *Becoming a Writer*. Choose a text as a suitable model, select a passage from it and imitate it. Write on a different topic, but use the same form.

If the passage has two paragraphs, write two paragraphs. If the first paragraph has two sentences of nine and fourteen words respectively, write two sentences of those lengths. If the first sentence has a comma after the fifth word, so should yours. If the first word has three syllables, begin your piece with three syllables. If the third word is a verb, make your third word a verb, and so on.

You have to use your judgement to decide just how precisely pupils should imitate the original. How far you go will depend to some extent on pupils' grammatical understanding. I would urge you, though, to imitate in as much detail as possible. Paradoxically, the more prescriptive you are, the more lateral the pupils' thinking will be and the more liberated their writing will become.

The aim here is not to produce a pastiche. It is to get the pupils writing in new ways. The exercise provides a very concrete way of introducing new styles. Use the opportunities for collaborative work – in pairs and together as a class. And try it at least once yourself.

FORENSIC LINGUISTICS

Please don't be put off by the title. This is, at least in essence, a simple idea and you can make the tasks very accessible.

A group of writers meet for a conference. A body is found. The only clue is that the murderer has dropped a piece of writing at the scene of the crime. You have samples of writing from each of the suspects. On the basis of those samples, who would you say wrote the text on the incriminating piece of paper?

Not very believable, I know – but you're not asking anyone to believe it, really. What you do want is for pupils in their search for clues to look very carefully at the language of the texts they have been provided with.

The first time I did this, I gave the pupils not only samples of primary text but also biographical information about the writers. That was a mistake: it led to rather generalized discussion based purely on content. Without the background information, pupils start to focus on stylistics much more quickly (e.g. 'She always begins her poems with "I"').

I designed this initially as a task to develop reading. I subsequently found that asking pupils to write a report of their findings produced valuable pieces of writing for meeting assessment objectives concerned with knowledge about language (KAL).

I find that the task works best using poems, though it could be done with prose. I recommend having four suspects, one of whom produces text easily distinguished from the text dropped at the scene of the crime.

AUTHOR STUDY

Teachers have often used author studies – in which pupils read several texts by one author and often some background information about the author as well – as a way of teaching reading. It can, however, also be used as a means of teaching writing. In this case the objective is not to discover what, for example, that author has to say about certain subjects or what the reader thinks of the author's work. It is instead to learn how to write like the author.

Pupils read texts (whether whole works or selected passages) by a particular author, looking for characteristics of their work. It helps if they have done the kind of tasks outlined in Ideas 77 and 78.

You can teach the necessary stylistics through exercises in sorting, counting, and selecting. For example, in the selected passage which words does the author use to help you visualize the subject? Which ten words most convey the mood – or the author's opinion? What's the average length of the author's sentences? The longest, the shortest?

Note that pupils can often do such exercises with incomplete comprehension. And that doing such exercises and discussing their findings can help to improve that comprehension. Consequently, you can use the task to introduce certain authors earlier in the curriculum than you would normally do and help move pupils on to more challenging authors.

The point, however, is to develop their writing. There are four types of task you can set.

1 Write a list of points or questions called 'How to recognize the work of X'.
2 Write a list of tips or suggestions called 'How to write like X'.
3 Write a passage in the style of X.
4 What features characterize (or, less abstractly, do you expect to find in) a typical passage by X?

There is considerable flexibility in this task as regards the level of work and extent (i.e. the amount of text(s) the pupils read). Combine extensive reading (reading as much text as possible within the time available) with intensive teaching of short – perhaps very short – passages.

One-offs and fillers

BALLOON DEBATE

Though only a filler this idea helps to improve pupils' general knowledge. And it gives you a chance to counter those critics who argue that we don't do enough to teach about famous people like Nelson.

If you're not familiar with balloon debates, let me explain. There's a group of people in a balloon. All of them happen to be famous. Nelson Mandela's in there, so too is Florence Nightingale – as well as Wayne Rooney, of course. Unfortunately, the balloon is losing height. Someone will have to be thrown overboard. Whoever that person is will of course be lost to society. Each character has the chance to make a speech to explain how and why they are too valuable to lose. Then the audience votes and someone is thrown out. But the balloon continues to lose height. Each person is given a brief opportunity to add to his or her defence before the audience votes again. And so on until there is only one person left in.

It's best, by the way, if each balloon has only a few people in it, otherwise the later rounds get a little tedious. Give pupils time to research and prepare properly – including, preferably, homework time. It's important to get some detail into the speeches rather than just generalized ideas. Remind them to hold a few ideas back for later rounds.

Before the debates, pupils make preparatory notes and write draft speeches. Afterwards they can make a display of characters' speeches or, more quickly, of pupils' views ('I think the person who should be kept is. . .because').

Most of the writing that pupils do in school is in the first or third person. For a change, let's do a piece in the second person.

Discuss the ways in which we commonly use 'you' and 'your'. Think about the texts that are characterized by the second person. The language of argument, for example: 'You said. . .yes, you did. . .. You always. . .that's the problem with you.' Love too: think of love songs, valentines and also of elegies.

Collect catch phrases ('You heard it here first'). Think of famous texts ('Thou art in heaven'). Don't forget the second person plural ('Come gather all ye miners'). Look up first lines of poems. Look at the lyrics of songs like 'Positively 4th Street' and 'Wedding Song' on Bob Dylan's (searchable) website (www.bobdylan.com).

Now write a text in which the second person predominates. It isn't necessary, of course, to prohibit any use of the first or third person. Many texts – Jesus's Sermon on the Mount and Mark Antony's 'Friends, Romans, countrymen' speech in Act 3 Scene 2 of *Julius Caesar* – depend for their effect on the contrast. But by beginning every (or at least most) lines or sentences with 'You', pupils can often create texts of great power, intensity or pathos. Which is more than can be said of most fillers.

WRITING IN THE SECOND PERSON

YOUR IDEAL ROOM

I am not very keen on one-offs. I am mindful of Pam Czerniewska's acerbic comment in her book, *Learning About Writing*: 'Schools, where the display and analysis of decontextualized knowledge is practised, develop learners who are able to perform well on tasks requiring decontextualized skills. But there is no evidence that this is a general intellectual ability underpinning other abilities' (p. 9).

But I do recognize that sometimes you need just to fill a gap. So here's a filler that seems to work. I used to play a video about four designers who were each briefed to create the perfect room. They came up with strikingly different designs. I used this as a stimulus to discussion and then asked pupils to draw and write about their ideal rooms.

When I moved schools I lost the video, but I found it didn't much matter. I collected photos (my own, postcards, illustrations) of all kinds of rooms and pretty rapidly built up a diverse gallery of designs. This provided a starting point but what really stimulated discussion were pupils' descriptions of, and comments about, rooms that they liked or disliked. After that we discussed, just a little, our ideal rooms and I put some of the key concepts on the board: shape; colour; texture; materials.

The pupils' main task was to draw their perfect rooms and to supplement their drawings with writing about what they wanted to tell me that wasn't already clear from the pictures – and also about why they had designed the rooms in the way they did.

Give pupils a crossword grid from a newspaper. Ignore the clues. Announce a theme (e.g. buildings). Pupils have to complete the grid by writing in words connected to the theme.

Take a sentence from a novel. Write out the first letter of each word. For example, my previous sentence becomes 'W O T F L O E W'. Pupils each make a sentence using words beginning with those letters and in the same order (for example, 'Walking over the footbridge. . .'). Read out several of these sentences along with the original: who can guess which was the original?

Choose a word of a certain number of letters (let's say five). Write it on the board. For example, 'ABOUT'. Pupils have to think of a word that (a) contains the same number of letters, (b) comes later in the alphabet and (c) has at least one letter in common with the previous word. For example, 'BROTH' also has an 'O' as its third letter. You may gradually make the game more complex. Give a bonus point if the word begins with the very next letter of the alphabet (here, 'CRUSH" rather than 'DRAFT'). Award two bonus points if it begins with the same letter. If the word shares more than one letter with the previous one, award a point for each such letter.

Choose a prefix ('dis-'). How many words can pupils think of with that prefix within a given time limit? Ditto suffixes.

CONSTRUCTING TEXTS BY PLAYING GAMES

Write a story – preferably in a single sentence – in which the first letters of words follow the order of the alphabet ('A beautiful Cornish diva. . .')

Play a game called Headlines invented by David Parlett (see *The Penguin Book of Word Games*, from which I have borrowed all of these games). Write a personal description (e.g. 'Infamous'). Fold over the paper and pass it on. Write the type of person ('plumber'). Fold over, pass on. Write a verb in the present tense ('conceals'). The verb needs to be transitive (the meaning of 'transitive' is in practice not difficult to convey). The fourth stage is to write the object of the verb ('professor') and fifth is to give the location. So you get something like 'INFAMOUS PLUMBER CONCEALS PROFESSOR IN FRIDGE'.

Take a word (e.g. 'conjure'). Write a telegram in which the words take their first letters in sequence from the key word: CAN'T OPERATE NIGHTLY: JUST UNDID ROYAL ELBOW. (When I used this at the start of my career, everyone knew what a telegram was. Now it needs explanation.)

Take the first stanza of a poem. Put the words into an alphabetical list. Give the list to the pupils, ask them to construct the stanza. Note that it doesn't matter (and might be desirable) if some of the words are unfamiliar. Experiment by giving information about punctuation marks ('You're allowed three commas') and by replacing one word with a wild card.

Assessment

THE PLACE OF ASSESSMENT

I have placed this section towards the end of the book. That seems natural (after all, you need pupils to produce written work before you can assess it) – but we need to keep in mind that in two ways assessment comes *before* teaching.

First, before teaching a class you need to consider existing assessment data on the pupils and use it to inform your decisions about what and how to teach. Second, you need to consider before you set a piece of work how it is going to be assessed.

In many cases you'll want not only to decide how the work will be assessed, but also to explain that to the pupils. If they know where the goal is, then they're more likely to score.

I say 'in many cases' rather than 'always' because awareness of assessment objectives can distract pupils from the actual writing. It can cause pupils to restrict their imagination and take fewer risks in their writing. As always, there is no substitute for exercising one's judgement based on a knowledge of the pupils.

The important point is to think of assessment not as the final stage of the process of teaching writing, but as part of a continuing cycle.

If you try listing *all* the criteria by which pupils' work may be marked, you'll find it's a very long list. If you try applying all the criteria at once, assessment is likely to be difficult for you and unhelpful – because unfocused – for pupils.

Relax. Specify a few criteria for each task. Suppose, for example, you set six pieces of written work each marked against three criteria. That will produce a record of 18 marks for each pupil. That's a pretty rich store of data with which to analyse each pupil's work. Of course, you may repeat some of the criteria. Even so, it's still quite easy to cover, say, ten criteria in six pieces of work.

As subject coordinator for English, I introduced a system of marking each key piece of work against three or four criteria, each listed on a cover slip for pupils and each marked out of four. For example, a piece of original writing was marked for (i) imaginativeness, (ii) vocabulary and (iii) spelling. The cover slip for the media task, on the other hand, read:

Understanding of texts	0	1	2	3	4
Use of detail	0	1	2	3	4
Clarity of explanation	0	1	2	3	4

The teacher would ring the appropriate scores and add a relevant comment, preferably including advice for improvement.

We found that marking became more focused and, praise be, much quicker. We also found that pupils could use the system to self-assess. The biggest boon of all was that this system made my comments at parents' evenings much more precise. A glance at my mark book produced an informative profile of the pupil's work. Though it sounds utopian to say it, reports started to write themselves.

There must be some catch – in education, there always is – but I haven't found it yet.

SELF-ASSESSMENT

Self-assessment by pupils is now generally seen as a Good Thing. Well, I certainly don't think it's a bad one. It encourages pupils to reflect on their own work. It indicates how well they understand what they're trying to achieve. It can raise issues for the teacher to focus on. Perhaps the greatest benefit of self-assessment is that it can create genuine dialogue between pupils and teachers.

Self-assessment can inform the teacher too. I still remember a girl called Megan writing in her coursework folder that she deserved the top grade because 'although no single piece meets all of the criteria, the folder as a whole does'. Blow me down if she wasn't right. Would I have noticed it if she hadn't pointed it out? Maybe, maybe not.

But self-assessment doesn't always work. It can become boringly routine and merely procedural. To work well it needs to be done in the right spirit. Show that you do listen to pupils' observations. Wherever possible, respond to the points that pupils have made. Each time your comment picks up on a pupil's comment, you help to re-enforce the purpose of self-assessment.

Unsurprisingly, teachers like to use symbols as a shorthand when marking. Mine wrote 'sp', 'p' and 'gr' in the margin a lot. I did work out what they stood for, but I'm not sure anyone ever bothered to explain them.

Teachers do need to explain their symbols. But often explanation is not enough. Pupils need to remember symbols clearly enough to be able to interpret them instantly, otherwise marking is largely a waste of time.

Interpretation is hardest when pupils move, for whatever reason, between teachers. It is easiest when groups of teachers have a stock of symbols in common. Which shouldn't, after all, be difficult to arrange – though it may call for a little bit of dictatorship. Get pupils to staple a list of marking symbols into their exercise books.

Whatever your school decides on as its standard symbols, I suggest that they include smilies and grumpies. They're clear, pupils like them – and oddly enough the older pupils get, the more they seem to like them.

IDEA

88

USING SYMBOLS FOR MARKING

CROSS-HATCHING

You want to assess pupils' written work in detail, including such matters as spelling and punctuation. And you want to be seen not to have skimped. But you don't want to mark every point on every page. That kind of marking takes too long and pupils fail to learn anything from it other than, perhaps, discouragement. What's the solution?

Select a passage from the pupil's work. Indicate the start and finish of the passage with a '#'. Mark intensively within that passage and more impressionistically outside. Explain to pupils what you're doing. Do it each time. Ideally, arrange for colleagues to do the same. That way, everyone knows where they stand.

When pupils get their work back, insist that they look at the cross-hatched passage in detail and ask about anything they want to query. Before pupils hand in their next pieces of work, insist that they go back through previous cross-hatched passages and use your corrections to help them check their work.

I can't remember who I stole this idea from, but to whoever it was I am extremely grateful.

Work does not always need to be complete before you begin to assess it. Formative assessment of unfinished work is one of the great arts of teaching.

And it is very much an art. I've watched some very bad examples of teachers discussing work in progress. Don't treat a pupil's work as your own. Remember that the pupil will have a perspective on his or her work. Get them talking. What problems are they encountering? Where do they want to take the work next? What options can they see? Above all, avoid doing the work for them: the important thing is not for the work to be done properly, but for *the pupil* to learn to do the work properly.

One of the most valuable aspects of the art of formative assessment is indicating when a pupil needs to take things further. Often when young writers are writing well, they tend – either out of modesty or lack of confidence – to settle for good work when they could achieve something even better. This is a major difference between school pupils and professional writers. When the latter find a technique that works they milk it for all it's worth and when they hit upon interesting material they mine it as deeply as possible. Sometimes you can narrow the gap between pupil and professional writer simply by saying to the former, 'That is really promising, don't leave it at that, PUSH IT FURTHER!'

DESIGNING ASSESSMENT QUESTIONS

Decide on the purpose of your questions. For example: to check, develop, or apply pupils' understanding; to provide assignments for classwork or homework; to provide a summative assessment; to provide practice of exam or test questions.

Distinguish between closed and open questions. The former have limited ranges of answers and produce very short replies. Open questions, which yield a wider range of possibilities and encourage extended answers, are more useful for developing pupils' writing.

Use as wide a range of interrogatives as possible: Who? What? When? Where? Which? How? Why?

Ensure that you distinguish between 'how' and 'why' questions. This sounds elementary, yet I've frequently seen questions that should be 'how' questions written as 'why' questions instead. Use 'How?' when you mean 'In what way?'. Reserve 'Why?' for asking 'For what reason?', 'With what purpose?' and 'On what grounds?'

Step your questions, i.e. begin with simple ones and put the harder ones lower down the list.

Use the following checklist to help you extend the range of questions. Have you included questions, where possible, on:

o similarities *and* differences; comparisons *and* contrasts?
o past, present *and* future?
o people, objects *and* processes?
o the detail *and* the big picture?

The key point is to explain that it is possible to know a subject well but do badly in an exam or test. These test both understanding of the subject and exam technique.

We all know that the most important thing is to answer the question. The problem is that simply telling pupils that has little effect. 'Of course I'd answer the question,' they think, 'why wouldn't I?'

It helps to go a little further and explain that pupils often answer either (a) the question they thought they were going to get or (b) the one they hoped they'd get.

On one memorable occasion nearly every member of an exam class I taught chose to ignore the actual wording on a past paper that we were using as a mock exam and to answer some questions they had in mind instead. The questions were similar, but not the same. I well remember marking the essays because it didn't take much time. I gave each one zero and at the bottom of each script wrote the question that I guessed the pupil had, as it were, invented – to which their response was, 'Fair cop!'

Usually things are not so dramatic. But after a test or mock exam it is usually possible to read out (anonymously) selected sentences or paragraphs that are clearly not aimed at the question the pupils have been asked – and to ask the class to try to guess what other question the writer must have had in mind.

Teach pupils to read questions more than once, underline key words, think about the key words, plan their answers around the key words, use the key words in their answers (especially in the opening sentences of paragraphs), and check at the end to make sure that they've covered the key words.

ANSWERING EXAM QUESTIONS

TEACHING THE USE OF TIME IN EXAMS

There are two key aspects to pupils' management of time in exams and tests. The first involves allocating time according to the mark scheme. If there are two questions, one worth 20 marks and one worth 40, is it really a good idea to spend equal amounts of time on them? In the run up to the exam, do some simple calculations on the board to show ways of allocating time.

The second aspect involves pupils setting aside time for checking their answers – and, if they finish early, to use all of the available time for checking (see Idea 46).

It's important to get pupils thinking about time and to understand that there are decisions to be made. I used the word 'management' in the first line above. Pupils do not necessarily think of themselves as managing time, especially in exams (which they tend to see as something being inflicted on them, rather than as something they can control). Teaching pupils to use time effectively is therefore a matter of inculcating an attitude of taking responsibility.

I taught one boy who took the business of time allocation so seriously that he would stop writing an answer at a pre-ordained time, even if he were halfway through a sentence. That seemed to be a little extreme (!) – but a lot better than the opposite.

Resources and teacher development

You need some school dictionaries, which I suggest you choose from those published by Oxford University Press (visit www.oup.co.uk/oxed/dictionaries). It helps, for teaching dictionary skills and language awareness, to have a class set or at least sets for use in small groups.

You need at least one adult dictionary. As well as an OED (for electronic access, visit www.oup.co.uk) it is helpful to have others, for example, Encarta, Webster's, Chambers – at least in the library. Teach pupils to compare dictionaries. The differences show that dictionaries involve judgement. A dictionary is not an incontrovertible authority, however much we might like to think it is.

If you haven't yet got an *ACE Spelling Dictionary*, try to get hold of a copy. It's the perfect answer to the pupil who points out (logically enough) that dictionaries are no use for looking up spellings because you first have to know how a word is spelt in order to find it. With ACE you need know only which letter a word begins with and how many syllables it has. It's one of the most ingenious and useful reference books I've ever come across.

More sophisticated is the *New Oxford Dictionary for Writers and Editors*. This doesn't aim to cover as much ground as the OED. It concentrates on those things that writers are most likely to want to check – the spelling of tricky words, for example, or the distinctions between confusables. It is designed to be consulted quickly so as not to interrupt the flow of writing.

Dictionaries of specific aspects of English are great for teaching with. I recommend having a tray containing as many of the following as your school can afford: dictionaries of first names, surnames, place names, idioms, slang, catch phrases, synonyms, and clichés. Examples of each of these are available from Oxford University Press (www.oup.co.uk) and/or Penguin (www.penguin.co.uk).

If possible, add an etymological dictionary (e.g. Bloomsbury's *Dictionary of Word Origins*) for teaching where words have come from and how their meaning has changed. Supplement this with OUP's *Dictionary of Foreign Words and Phrases*, which deals with those items – invariably perplexing to pupils – that have been incorporated directly into English from other languages (e.g. 'pro bono', 'cum laude').

You can use these resources not only to answer specific needs (a pupil wanting to invent a character's name, for example) but also to encourage pupils to play with language. It's important not to be too inflexible about how pupils use these books. If a pupil goes to look up one thing and ends up looking at lots of other entries as well, that's a welcome sign of curiosity or responsiveness.

Good reference books support teaching in general, especially work on language awareness. They also provide opportunities for 'filler' activities. Five minutes spent looking up the derivations of surnames can be great fun. And simply from the point of view of general knowledge, it's good that pupils know such books exist.

SPECIALIZED DICTIONARIES

MATERIALS

Writing isn't always easy to accommodate in classrooms and timetables. Watch the behaviour of adults who write a lot – their behaviour is often very different from the way we expect pupils to write in class. To some extent school is bound to be artificial and inflexible, but there are some ways in which we can replicate the conditions in which people choose to write out of school.

For example, the provision of materials. I write a good deal. For some purposes, I use a pencil. For others, I use a pen – I associate various kinds of pens with various tasks. I word-process most of my extended writing, though the journal I keep is handwritten and most of the very early stages of drafting any extended document I do on paper. I use different kinds of paper for different kinds of writing – a notebook, a jotting pad, scrap paper and new A4. I enjoy browsing in stationery and office supply shops. I like having various pieces of equipment close to hand – a stapler, a steel ruler (it has to be steel), etc.

These preferences might be idiosyncratic – but having preferences of some sort and liking to have a range of implements available is typical of writers. In school we often make do with a very restricted range of materials – a pupil may well use the same writing tool all day and write either in exercise books or paper all of one size. Experiment with building up a stock of materials. Add things even if you're not sure why. Though stationery can be expensive, some materials – scrap paper, superfluous diaries, used envelopes, and so on – are free or inexpensive. Ideally, create a writer's corner with a few trays nearby.

In my experience, primary school teachers do this better than secondary teachers, but the needs or preferences of secondary school pupils are pretty similar.

Sandy Brownjohn's books – published by Hodder in omnibus form as *To Rhyme or Not to Rhyme?* – provide mountains of imaginative yet practical ideas for creative writing, supported by examples from the work of children she has taught. Most of her work seems to have been with the older years of primary schools, but many of her ideas can be used with other age groups – some might even appeal to you as a writer yourself. My favourite is 'Last Will and Testament', which requires pupils to write poetic wills in which they decide not only which tangibles to leave ('I leave my Ferrari to Frankie') but also which intangibles ('To Jonty I leave equanimity').

In the same tradition is Fred Sedgwick's *Teaching Literacy*, which includes poetry and prose and again has plentiful examples of pupils' own work. Sedgwick's book (which I referred to in Idea 66) is more discursive than Brownjohn's. Although it isn't set out as a series of instructions on a lesson-by-lesson basis, it is very concrete and requires little effort to be converted into one's own lessons.

What I like most about Brownjohn and Sedgwick is that both draw on their teaching experiences in inspiring ways. In contrast, I have not found nearly as much inspiration on the Internet as I'd expect. One website, however, does attract me – despite its terrible name – as a source both of intelligent thinking about the teaching of writing and of practical examples. See Kim's Korner for Teacher Talk: www.kimskorner4teachertalk.com/writing/menu.html

Frank Smith's *Writing and the Writer* is the best book I know for teachers about writing. It was published in 1982 and so does not take account of recent research, but it remains a perceptive, sophisticated, concise account of how we write. (Readers already familiar with the book will have noticed its influence in this one – for which I make no apology!) Smith's book is out of print, but it's well worth trying to acquire a copy through secondhand Internet sites such as Abe Books (www.abebooks.co.uk) or eBay (www.ebay.co.uk). It won't give any lesson plans but it will provide you with an overview of the nature and processes of writing and their implications for teaching.

Nigel Harwood is a contemporary expert on ELT. In his work he identifies two paradigms that have been very influential in teaching writing – the process approach, exemplified by Frank Smith's work, and the genre approach adopted by educators such as David Wray (see Idea 26). These paradigms lie behind much of the book you are reading now.

Harwood, however, proposes a third approach – the 'sample approach'. This approach is based on providing pupils not with model texts, but with samples of flawed texts – more precisely, texts that have some merit but which contain some of the typical weaknesses of pupils' own writing. Teacher and the pupils work together to assess the samples and improve them.

I would have grave concerns about including misspellings and confusables among the flaws contained in such samples. That stipulation apart, the approach seems to me a stimulating extension of the type of thinking set out in Ideas 8 and 24. For more detail and Harwood's rationale, visit his website (http://privatewww. essex.ac.uk/~nharwood). See especially his paper on the sample approach, published in 2000 and available under 'Publications'.

For my first few years of teaching I wrote nothing beyond what was required for everyday living. My intellectual energies were focused almost entirely on teaching.

When I started to extend my writing, it was in small-scale, low-key ways. I started keeping a journal. I wrote a review for a county teaching magazine that a group of colleagues knocked out on a primitive word processor.

I did this for my own benefit. The odd thing was, though, that I found that as my writing developed it started to inform my teaching. In particular, it helped me to help individual pupils with their writing. By some mysterious process I developed greater empathy for what was going on in pupils' heads as they wrote. Some of my best moments as a teacher have been when I have sat down with pupils, read their drafts, made guesses about what problems they were encountering and where they were thinking of taking their writing next. I remember saying to one pupil, 'I know you've chosen to write this, but I don't think that this is what you want to write at all. I sense that what you really want to write is. . .' and she said, 'How on earth did you know that?' My intuition wasn't foolproof, but it certainly developed.

How do you develop yourself as a writer? Well, you don't have to be Dostoyevsky. Writing a journal helps, as does a regular correspondence, though I think it probably needs to be by letter rather than email.

There is a fantastic variety of workshops and courses available. See the section on creative writing courses in A&C Black's annual publication, *Writers' & Artists' Yearbook*. Many literary festivals provide writing workshops – visit the British Council website (www.britishcouncil.org/arts-literature-literary-festivals.htm). When I went on a weekend poetry-writing course run by the Taliesin Trust I was amazed to find how much my writing developed through working alongside fellow enthusiasts with the guidance of expert tutors.

SELF-DEVELOPMENT

Dear Trainee or Newly Qualified Colleague,

I hope that you enjoy teaching in general and teaching writing in particular. I hope too that this book proves helpful and that you use — or, as teachers tend to do, adapt — at least a few of the ideas.

I have saved the most important idea until last. This book is based on a certain view of pupils. It sees them as people who require teaching — they do not know everything already — but who are not empty vessels. They come to the classroom with words, meanings and ideas in their heads — and feelings too.

Whatever you want to do with your pupils' thinking — harness it, develop it, challenge it, correct it — the important point is to <u>interact</u> with it. If you do that you will be taking one giant step down the road to good practice in the teaching of writing.

Best wishes,

Anthony Haynes

REFERENCES

John Ayto (ed.), *The Bloomsbury Dictionary of Word Origins*. Bloomsbury, 2001.

Howard S. Becker, *Writing for Social Scientists*. University of Chicago Press, 1986.

Ronald Blythe, *Akenfield*. London: Penguin, 2005.

Dorothea Brande, *Becoming a Writer*. London: Macmillan, 1986.

Sandy Brownjohn, *To Rhyme or Not to Rhyme?* Hodder Murray, 1994.

Mary Chamberlain, *Fenwomen*. Virago, 1977.

Pam Czerniewska, *Learning about Writing*. Blackwell, 1992.

Ruth Finnegan (ed.), *The Penguin Book of Oral Poetry*. Penguin, 1982.

Natalie Goldberg, *Writing Down the Bones*. Shambhala, 1986.

Thomas Gray, 'Elegy Written in a Country Church Yard' in Christopher Ricks (ed.), *The Oxford Book of English Verse*. OUP, 1999.

George V. Higgins, *On Writing*. Henry Holt, 1990.

Margaret Langdon, *Let the Children Write*. Longmans, 1961.

Maureen Lewis and David Wray, *Writing Frames*. University of Reading, Reading & Language Information Centre, 1996.

Jan Mark, *Thunder and Lightnings*. Kestrel, 1986.

David Moseley, *ACE Spelling Dictionary*. Learning Development Aids, 1986.

New Oxford Dictionary for Writers and Editors. OUP, 2005.

George Orwell, *Down and Out in Paris and London*. Penguin, 2003.

David Parlett, *The Penguin Book of Word Games*. Harmondsworth, 1981.

Madsen Pirie, *How to Win Every Argument*. Continuum, 2006.

Fred Sedgwick, *Teaching Literacy*. Continuum, 2004.

Frank Smith, *Writing and the Writer*. London: Heinemann Education Books, 1982.

Jennifer Speake, *The Oxford Dictionary of Foreign Words and Phrases*. OUP, 2005.

Francis Spufford (ed.), *The Chatto Book of Cabbages and Kings*. Chatto and Windus, 1989.

J.M. Synge, *The Aran Islands*. Penguin, 1992.

Keith Topping, *Thinking Reading Writing*. Continuum, 2002.

Robin Williams, *The Non-designer's Design Book* (2nd edn). Peachpit Press, 2004.

Writers' & Artists' Yearbook. A&C Black, annually.